Super Survivors: Citizens of the World and Planet Earth - Super Sobrevivientes: Ciudadanos del Mundo y del Planeta Tierra

J C Doyle and Kevin Levin

Published by Business EdPublisher, 2018.

While every precaution has been taken in the preparation of this book, the publisher assumes no responsibility for errors or omissions, or for damages resulting from the use of the information contained herein.

SUPER SURVIVORS: CITIZENS OF THE WORLD AND PLANET EARTH - SUPER SOBREVIVIENTES: CIUDADANOS DEL MUNDO Y DEL PLANETA TIERRA

First edition. December 14, 2018.

Copyright © 2018 J C Doyle and Kevin Levin.

ISBN: 978-1393213512

Written by J C Doyle and Kevin Levin.

Also by J C Doyle

Super Survivors: Citizens of the World and Planet Earth - Super Sobrevivientes: Ciudadanos del Mundo y del Planeta Tierra

Watch for more at www.josephjcharles.com.

Also by Kevin Levin

Watch for more at kevinlevinebooks.blogspot.com.

A todos los Tijuanenses, Haitijuanenses de la Frontera!

To all the citizens of Tijuana and those born on the border!

Super Survivors: Citizens of the World and Planet Earth

Super Sobrevivientes: Ciudadanos del Mundo y del Planeta Tierra

"Thanks to all the Tijuanenses! Gracias a Todos los Tijuanenses!"

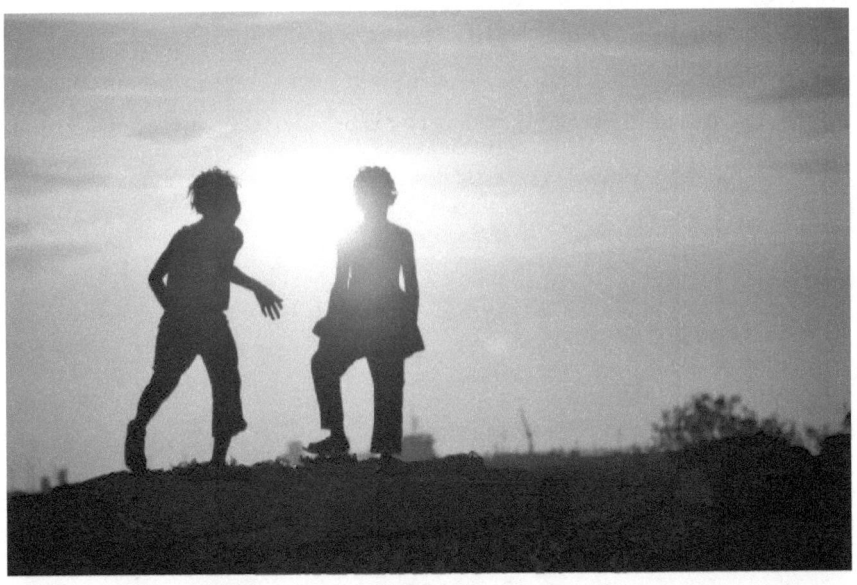

The Perilous and Treacherous Journey: Trek, Travels, and Stories of Unaccompanied Minors and Migrants From Haiti, Central America, Mexico, Asia, Africa, and Elsewhere Thru the U.S./Mexico Border.

by J C Doyle, Kevin Levin, and C D Laferrière. Editor/Curator: Joseph Charles

Copyright 2016. By J C Doyle, Kevin Levin and C D Laferrière

From the Mouths of Children: Haiti Quake and Hurricane Matthew Survivors Tell Their Own Stories

Fear and Prayer in Chaotic Times: The Traumatized Children Survivors of climate change, earthquake, and hurricane encounter migrants from all over the world at the US-Mexico border.

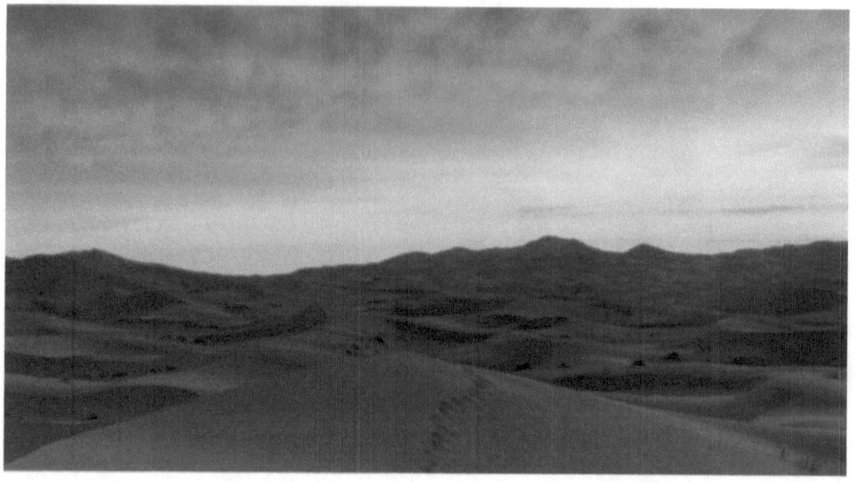

Surviving and Living in Chaotic Times under the Sun and Climate Change.

A Memoir of Survival and Desperate Journey across Parts of the Old and New Worlds

America is at a Crossroads! The Global Refugee and Migrants' Desperate Trek for a better life.

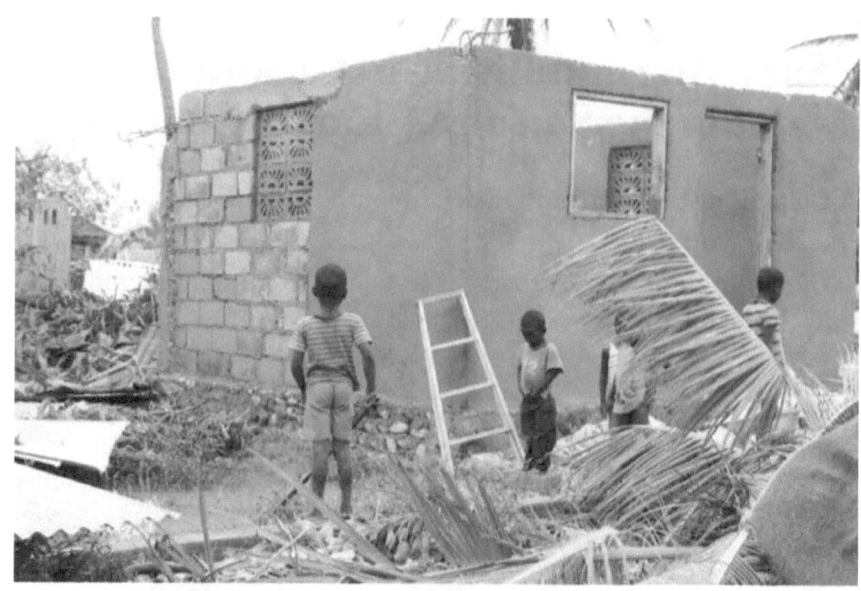

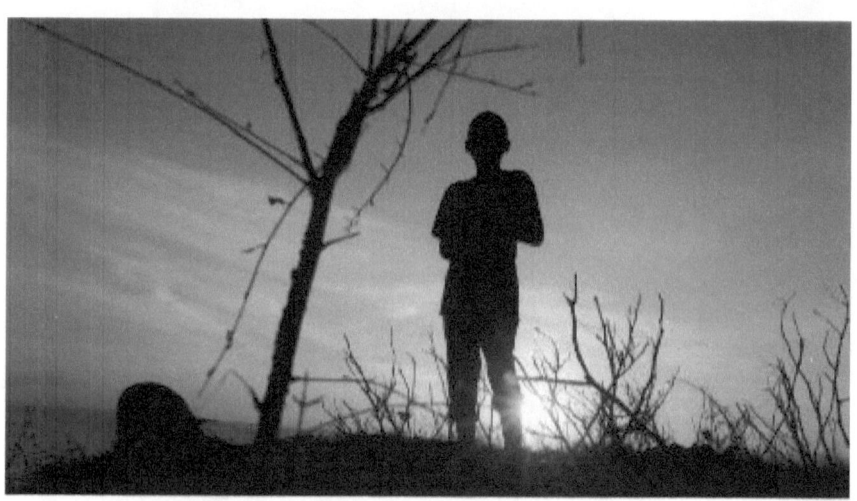

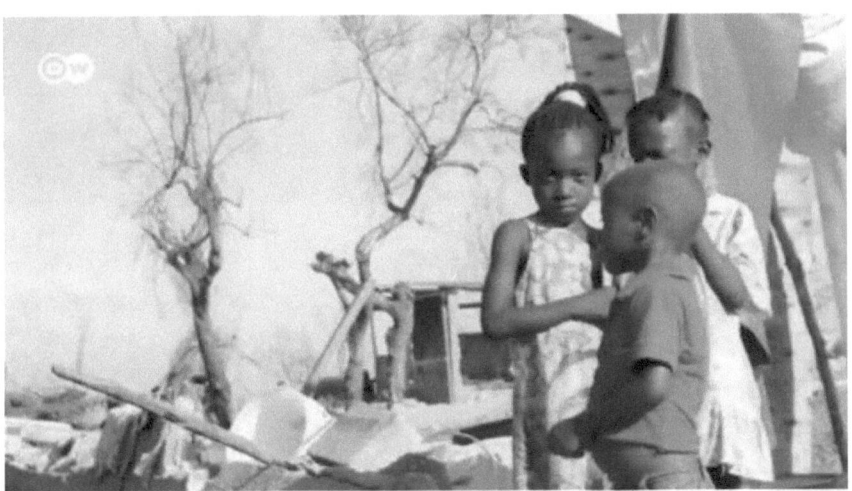

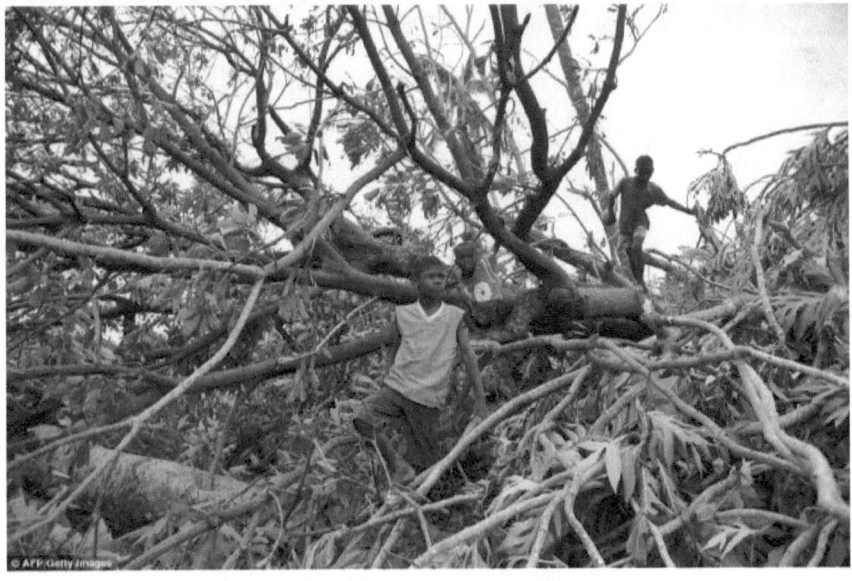

Chapter 1

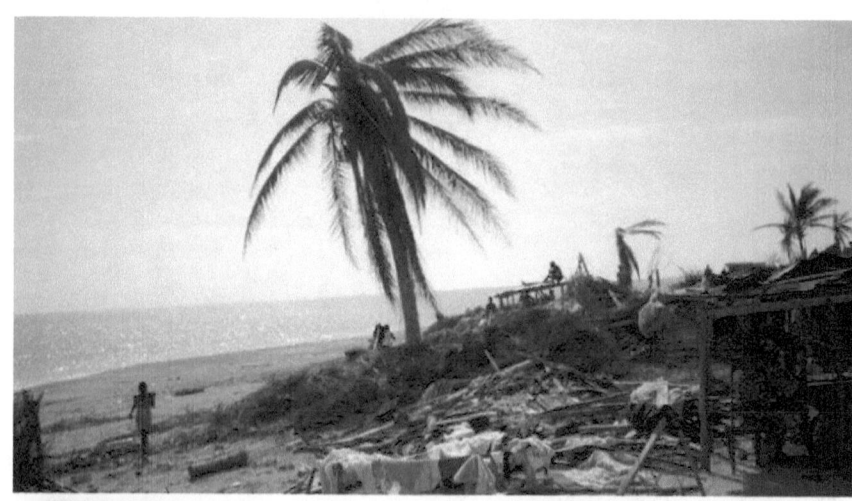

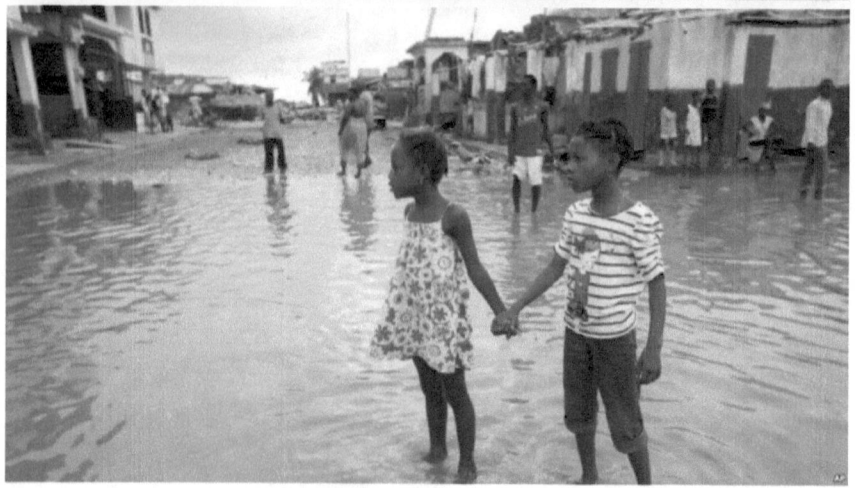

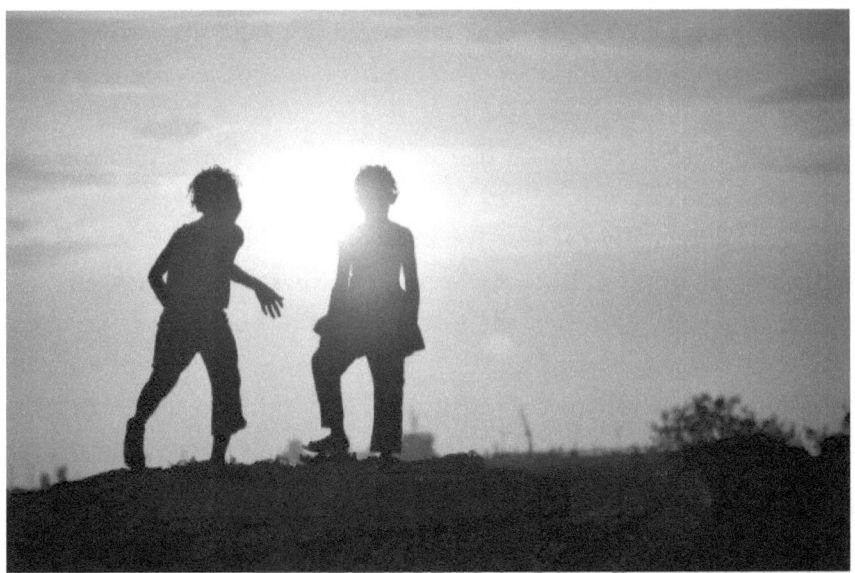

After the devastation caused by Hurricane Matthew in Jeremie and Les Cayes, Haiti on October 4, 2016, two young girls set out to explore what is left of their towns. They were determined to tell their stories to other kids all over the world. Their stories touched all the boys and girls living in the coastal areas that were mostly impacted by the category 4 hurricane, packing winds of 145 miles or (230 kilometers) per hour. From Les Anglais, Chantal, Aquin, Cavaillon, Port-Salut, Chardonières, Tiburon, Saint Louis du Sud to Dame Marie, Anse D'Hainault, Pestel, Moron, and Les Abricots, the young survivors resorted to storytelling as their only form of therapy. They are the eyewitnesses of the strong winds, pelting rain and flooding that took away their parents' homes, crops, and livestock. It was as if they witnessed the falling of the sky above their head.

After a sleepless night, Carline and Rose were thankful that they survived. They had found shelter in a nearby school. They spent the whole night praying and wondering whether they would make it the next day. They saw their mother praying hard to God. They saw their mother pulling Jesus down from heaven to ask for help. They closed their eyes for a short time, but they could not fall asleep. They were wondering and thinking about their father and brothers sheltered in a neighbor's home.

"Mom, I wonder how my dad and brothers are doing. Can you call Dad so we can talk to him?" asked Rose.

"Impossible. The phone is not working. No communication," replied their mother. Mrs. Aselòm knew what danger they may be facing. If it was up to her, she would prefer to be with her husband and sons. But she listened to Mr. Aselòm's advice. He did not want to lose his whole family to the hurricane. He decided to split it in two. He would take the boys to the neighbor's well-built home. They had to walk and cross two rivers to get there. And his wife would take the girls to the recently built school which was closer to the family's home.

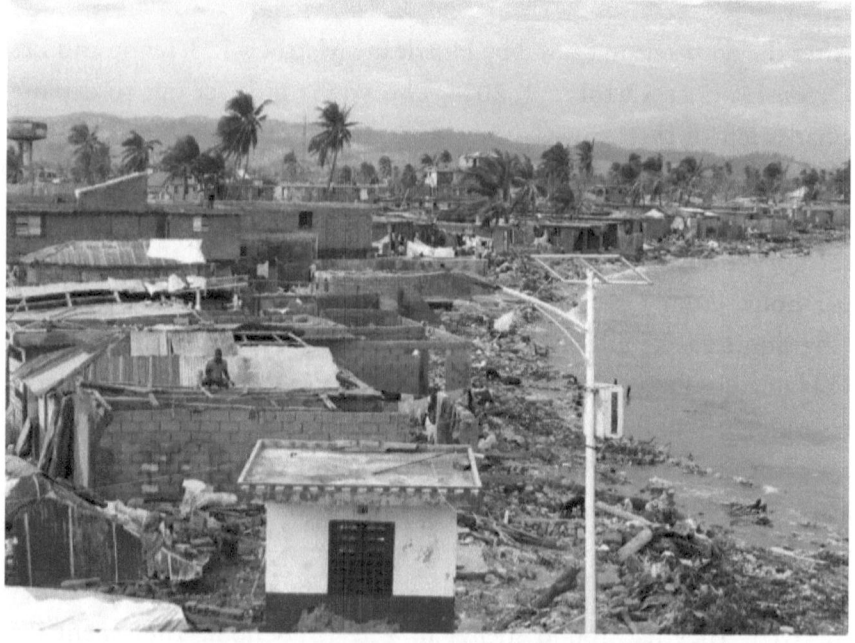

Carline and Rose were praying all night long with their mother. That was the only night they heard everybody praying. In the dark corner of the public school's classroom, they heard coconuts hitting the roof. They witnessed trunks of palm and coconut trees passing by the broken windows of the public school. Palm fronds were twisting as if they were dancing. They nearly touched the ground and rose back up like bamboos often do. Some coconut and palm trees withstood the 145 mph wind. Others did not. As the strong winds cracked, split them into two, and blew them away, they took other tall and powerful fruit trees such as breadfruit with them. The few breadfruits that remained standing became leafless. The next day, Carline and Rose witnessed the remaining breadfruit's branches giving praise to Mother Nature and the Cosmos. Boys and girls climbed the fallen breadfruit trees in search of fruits they could salvage. Then, the night of October 4, 2016 arrived.

"Oh God, help us live till tomorrow! Calm the storm. It's too noisy outside," prayed Carline.

"I pray for my school friends, my classmates. Oh God, be with them. Protect them. Protect my father. Protect my brothers. Protect my teachers in their homes. I do not know why they did not come to our public school. Is it because they thought their homes were safer and stronger? Please God, save our neighbors. Protect their huts," Rose was praying as she opened her eyes to see water pouring into the classroom.

Carline and Rose climbed on top of a long classroom bench. They saw other children sleeping on the floors of their classrooms. Some were naked and clothed in adult-sized T-shirts hanging below their knees. In those classroom shelters, they would be protected from flying debris such as tin-roofing sheets blown away by the strong winds.

"Mom, there is water in here," yelled Carline to her mother.

"Get on top of the bench. Stay there. Both of you!" ordered their mother.

Mrs. Aselòm took a break from praying only to give a hand to a pregnant woman whose own water broke. She was ready to give birth to a baby boy. More and more women joined to help this young woman who was giving birth to her first son. The ladies formed a circle to comfort and give her some privacy. They gave her a few sheets from the few supplies they carried for the night. All the men, except her husband, Dieusibon, moved to the adjoining classroom.

"Dieusibon, have you thought about a name for your baby boy?" asked Mrs. Aselòm who was trying to get the mother and the father's minds off their hectic situation. Mrs. Aselòm gave birth to 4 children. She knew what it was like to give birth during a hurricane.

"I had a name for him, but I think I am going to change it to a new one," replied Dieusibon, anxious but proud to-be-father.

"If it is ok with Toyo, my wife, I will call him '*Katastwòf Natirèl*.'"

The other women in the room laughed in unison, the same way most small merchants, *ti machann*, laugh in the open markets all over Haiti on a good market day. They were thinking about why Dieusibon could not give his newborn a French-sound name. They wanted to keep their cultural heritage.

"I hope that is going to be his nickname. I told you I want Jovani if I have a son and Jovanna if I have a daughter. Hold my back. I feel the need to push....Hold me tightly," yelled Toyo who was complaining of being too cold. A nearby mother of 6 children handed a blanket to her. And the women were quick to cover her legs.

In the midst of the strong winds, pelting rain and potential flooding, this young couple was ready to introduce their first son to the world, a world of quake, hurricanes, misery, pain, and hatred, but also a world of resilience, love, and fraternity.

Chapter 2

Carline and Rose got up early the day after Hurricane Matthew devastated Haiti's southern peninsula. They started thinking about the cities in Les Cayes and Jérémie, Grand'Anse. They used to accompany their parents to purchase and sell agricultural products in those places. They started walking in their own town to assess the devastation.

"Let's cross the water. Let's see what's going on in that store where our parents used to buy our uniforms," Carline said to Rose. Holding hands, they walked cautiously to avoid falling into a pothole caused by the ocean waves that visited downtown the night before.

"The store is flooded. Oh my God! That means the products and all other merchandise are destroyed. It's a total waste," responded Rose.

As they walked around, they witnessed more and more houses whose rooftops were blown away. Some were left abandoned. Their owners did not or could not find their way back to check on their homes and property. Others were being repaired with the metal sheets collected all over the city by their owners. Blown by the winds, some of these tin or metal sheets were like flying bombs, missiles and rockets the night the hurricane passed through the region.

"Look over here. People are trying to nail the metal sheets. That's the noise we hear. But the walls of the house are gone," said Carline.

"How about over there? The neighbors are talking to each other on the ruins of their former homes," said Rose. "Mothers and their children were collecting clothes and toys under the rubble."

In Port-Salut, Carline and Rose's Parents' friends, long-time fellow merchants, said that the mountains and hills were left denuded. The palm and coconut trees toppled by the hurricane lay on the grounds everywhere the girls went. They walked down to the seaside fishing neighborhood where the buildings were inundated and damaged.

"We have to go back. There is no way we will be able to cross. There may be nails in this water," said Carline.

"Children are crying everywhere we go. Some of them are naked. Their clothes were blown away and got deposited miles away. Their food supplies are destroyed. 'There is nothing left,' said a crying mother, with her hands on top of her head. Mothers did not have anything to feed their kids," said Rose.

Mothers and fathers became numb everywhere the two girls and their friends went. They witnessed and overheard the adults' complaints and signs of joy over small signs of survival. In most cases, those grownups were either crying over their massive loss in property, livestock, and future harvest.

Rose, Carline, and their friends walked along the inundated and muddy roads to listen to the stories of survival. They were shocked by what their town and significant landmarks have become.

"The noise was mind-blowing. It was so strong that trees and home foundation were being uprooted. From the cave where we were, we saw trunks of palm and coconut trees passing by. Tin sheets were flying like birds in the rain," said a group of men and women who had just descended from the mountain cave that served them as the only shelter. "If it was not for our neighbor who led us to the entrance of the cave on her property, we would not have survived. We would be blown away, sucked out of our home by the winds of the hurricane."

Two days after the passage of Hurricane Matthew, survivors were still hoping that humanitarian assistance would arrive. They needed shelter, reparation of their homes, basic food supplies such as cooking oil, beans, rice, cornmeal, cooking pans, and fire. They managed to survive on the meat of the collected dead animals blown away by the wind.

Carline, Rose and their friends stopped in another neighborhood to listen to the residents' stories.

"I do not have to say anything. Look at my house. It's flat. I lost everything. Two of my youngest sons were blown away by the winds. I lost my animals, my crops. I have nothing left. What you see are the ruins where my house and belongings stood," said 67-year-old Eliphat. "Even my clothes, mattresses, and bed are gone. What the wind did not take away, hungry protesters rioted over the slow reaction of the government and NGOs in delivering assistance."

"My wife and I lost everything. We lost our home. The ocean took it away with everything that was inside. We have nothing to live for. We are so far away from Port-au-Prince and the rest of the world," said Gesner, a 52-year-old businessman whose fishery was destroyed. "What are the residents of Jeremie going to eat?" he asked.

One of Carline's friends whose name was TiGrimo told her that he could take her to a coffin maker's workshop. The coffin maker became the busiest man in town. Emmanuel whose nickname was Boss Manno was in a sudden position to give jobs to all the new unemployed residents of Jeremie. TiGrimo's father was finally able to work with his compère, his buddy. Boss Manno became one of the top employers of Jeremie. He knew how to treat his clients. Through words of mouth, he was able to build his clientele all over the southern peninsula.

"Come on. Follow me. I will take you to my godfather's coffin workshop. He sent for my father yesterday because of all the demands he was getting. He said he used to sell 5 coffins, but after the hurricane, he did not have any stock. He had boards and saws. All he needed were men and women who wanted to work," said TiGrimo who got his name due to his light skin. He had the same skin color as his father, a common observation in Jeremie, Haiti.

Rose, Carline, and the other boys followed TiGrimo who walked three blocks away.

"This is where the noise was coming from. The coffin makers were busy nailing, sawing, and measuring boards."

Rose, Carline, and TiGrimo arrived at the coffin shop. They saw a lot of family members arriving to negotiate the purchase of a coffin. TiGrimo's father, GroGrimo, was busy working on the completion of a few coffins. He became the right-hand man for his compadre, his compère, his buddy from his adolescence years. Boss Manno grew up with GroGrimo. They played soccer and swam in the local rivers. They went to the beach together. They went to the same high school. Boss Manno and GroGrimo were always together. No wonder that Boss Manno came to rely on his best friend in a time of such busy labor.

"I would like to find two coffins for my family members," a skinny gentleman said to Boss Manno who had a long line of new customers.

"I am sorry for the pain and tribulations caused by Hurricane Matthew upon your family. I will do what I can to work with you. How can I help you?"

"My uncle sent me to talk to you about two coffins, a coffin for somebody who was as tall as me, and a baby coffin," said the delegate.

"What types of coffin do you want? Let's go to the back to see the types of coffins I have made over the years. I also have pictures I can show you. "

The skinny delegate followed Boss Manno to his display of coffins in the back of his shop. All the while, he was giving orders to his apprentice and employees.

"Feel free to tell me which one of these coffins you need. As far as the baby coffin, we can get it done for you in a matter of hours. It's so sad to hear what happened to your family members."

"I must tell you, Boss Manno, we have not found the bodies yet. We want to be ready in case we found the cadavers. The wind must have carried them far away. The authorities continue to recover bodies all along the mountains," said the skinny delegate with lots of sadness.

"Well, I thought you had already found the bodies," said Boss Manno with lots of surprise. "I will put your name on our list of coffins to be made."

"Can you tell me how much the two coffins will cost so we can get the money ready. The family has family members in Canada and the US. They are hoping to be able to communicate with them to request the amount," said the skinny delegate.

"The coffin that will fit your size will cost $ HT 700.00. I can always throw the small coffin on the price. I am touched by the disappearance of babies. That will be free," replied Boss Manno.

"What will happen to the cost if we can only find the baby?" asked the skinny delegate.

"Well, we will talk about it then. Come back to see me so we can talk. That's once you find the bodies. I have a lot of customers who are waiting for me. Give my condolences to your family members."

The skinny delegate left the coffin shop immediately.

Boss Manno was approached by a new family which was waiting for him. 4 members of the Bonbon family met him in his shop. Mr. Bonbon was the patriarch of the whole family. He was its main speaker. He was accompanied by his wife, two of his sons and 1 daughter. The Bonbons were a well-established Abricot Jeremie family whose sons and daughters live in Canada, France, the United States and Chili.

"Hello Mr. Bonbon. How can I help you? First, let me say I am sorry about your loss," said Boss Manno.

"We are here to see if we can purchase a coffin for my deceased father. Sweet Bonbon passed away last night. He survived the quake and the hurricane, but he could not survive the inundation and the loss of his crops. It was too much for him to understand the devastation of his home," replied the head of the family.

"Mr. Bonbon, this hurricane is one of the worst natural disasters I have ever lived through in this country. There are people who survived the 2010 quake and the cholera brought by the Nepalese UN troops, but they end up being ripped off from the face of this earth by Hurricane Matthew. There is not a Jeremie family that is not touched by this hazard. I will do my best to work with you."

"Thank you, Manno." Mr. Bonbon reached into his pocket and gave his father's measurement to Boss Manno.

And so went the whole day for Boss Manno who continued to see new clients. Making coffins in troubled times is a good business. Boss

Manno checked with some of his new employees before seeing his last customer.

"GroGrimo, how is everything going?" asked Boss Manno on his way to meet with his last customer.

"All is fine. We are completing 5 coffins in an hour. By this afternoon, we will have manufactured more than 60 coffins," replied GroGrimo, accompanied by TiGrimo and his friends. Boss Manno greeted his godson by passing his hand on his head.

"TiGrimo, has your dad been teaching you how to build coffins? You have not told me what you want to be when you grow up?" said Boss Manno.

"I want to be a pilot. I told you before," replied TiGrimo. Carline and Rose laughed.

"I may have forgotten. You can be whatever you set your mind on. As long as this coffin shop remains open, your dad and I will support you. Just pray for us. We are just a few hurricanes and quake away from death."

"Oh no. I do not want my dad to die. I do not want you to die either," said TiGrimo who became very emotional. He and his friends have seen so many dead bodies in the past few years.

"Come on, Manno. Do not start a life and death discussion with your godson and these kids," said GroGrimo who encouraged them to go see some of the coffins his co-workers have already completed.

"Go to the back of the shop. You will see some of our new coffins. We have a few small coffins. Do not be scared by them. Adults as well as kids are equal before death. Hurricanes and quakes make them all equal," said GroGrimo.

And TiGrimo, Carline, and Rose walked to the back of the shop. They were looking at the coffins displayed along the wall. They were most attracted to the small coffins displayed at the bottom of the tables, near the big coffins. In a matter of minutes, several shop workers entered to carry two coffins to their owners, waiting in the front. They had already paid for them. TiGrimo, Rose, and Carline stopped to look at the small coffins. They could not stop thinking about the small victims of the hurricane. They were thinking that some of them may be as old as they were.

All over the town, funeral ceremonies were being held. Men were busy digging holes all over the town and the countryside. There were men and women whose family members were completely wiped out by the hurricane. The few remaining neighbors of the nearby communities were left with the sordid, difficult task of burying the dead scattered all over the villages. Without any surviving family members looking for their loved ones and due to the fact that all communications were cut, there was no way of leaving all these bodies on the ground or around the water canals and rivers. Carline, Rose, TiGrimo and their friends were able to witness all those things.

Four days after the passage of the hurricane, family members started arriving from other far-away cities that were not touched by the hurricane. They could not stay away from their origin. That's why they did anything possible to travel back home. Despite the fact that La Dique Bridge was destroyed, they managed to pay people who would carry them on their back to cross the river. Their destination were those communities that were technically destroyed by the hurricane. Dame Marie, Les Irois, Les Abricots, Les Anglais, Moron, Port-Salut, Tiburon, Boucan, Chardonnière etc needed to hear from their sons and daughters living elsewhere or in the diaspora. The rising level of the sea brought inundation and major flooding to all of these coastal areas.

Boss Manno and GroGrimo knew they had clients who would come from all of these towns. They were willing to work with them to meet their coffin needs. As far as the kids, they were all too willing to visit the local funeral events.

There were so many missing individuals who were blown away by the hurricane that mourning came from all over. It was not difficult for Carline, Rose, and TiGrimo to find a funeral event to go to. After leaving the coffin shop, they walked down pass the local police station, jail and tribunal, all in various state of destruction. They were following the mourners of these funerals.

Chapter 3

The catholic Priest and the Mourners at the Funeral

Rose, Carline, and TiGrimo arrived at Mrs. De's home where two family members were killed by hurricane Matthew. They saw the priest of the local Catholic Church, Iglesia Divina, and a few nuns talking to the followers and comforting the mourners.

"Do not be desperate by the deaths, tribulations and calamities that hit our region. Just know you are not alone. The rest of the country stands with you. Hurricane Matthew did not attack the whole country," stated the priest in Spanish, French, and Creole. He ceased using Latin in his church for many years now. That was to the displeasure of many Catholic sympathizers and believers. Many of them still felt attacked by the Vatican edit banishing the use of Latin in local churches. Many of those old-timers still showed allegiance to Latin as their faith language through which they can have access to God through prayers and meditations.

"God abandoned us this time. With all the honor to you, Priest and nuns, I will say I have lost my faith. When I saw my friends being blown away, when I witnessed my plants being wiped out, when I have no home to live in, when my livestock is gone. What am I going to live on?" asked one of the mourners.

Around that time, a group of mourners started crying on the northern corner of the yard, under the mango tree. The rest of the mourners and family friends stayed under a tarp that was tied to the mango tree, the kitchen in the yard, and the balcony of the main house. The De Family was able to contact the few remaining and available mourners. Out of a group of 50 local mourners, the family was able to find only 10 of them who were willing to come to the wake. The others had too many problems to deal with. Either they had family members who were affected by Matthew hurricane or they were themselves victims. So the 10 mourners who went to The De Family's wake may have come because they had lost everything else. They came to support and comfort the family. They came to mourn their deceased family member. They came to cry over their years of poverty. They came to play domino, pay their last respect, drink tea and coffee. They came to reconnect with their friends and neighbors. It was an opportunity for them to find out who was still alive and who perished.

The coffee and tea waiters/waitresses walked around the large crowd to serve bread or alcoholic beverages from time to time. They took messages to the cooks in the kitchen. The domino players wanted everything. If there was coffee and tea available, that's what they wanted. But from time to time, they would ask for a few sips of alcohol. They wanted to scream and celebrate their win. They wanted to feel motivated to play and encourage the mourners. The teenagers and young kids came to the wake to learn a few songs. They also came to meet and greet their peers. Teenagers and adults came to find a date.

"Coffee. More coffee," yelled the players of one table. So the servers went to the kitchen to get more coffee. That night, the gravediggers came around to have some fun. They wanted to be around the living. All day long, they were working for the dead.

"Tea and bread. We are feeling cold out here in the rain," yelled the players at the table under the torn and almost leafless coconut tree. It was easier for the waiters to bring for the whole group of mourners who stood around the table. All of them will want to be served too. That required the servers to keep coming back with more beverage and pain. The domino players preferred to be served by the beautiful waitresses.

Yet, on the balcony, the young men and women stood around the many tables of domino where the mostly male players never ceased slamming the bones on the tables to the attraction and pleasures of the women singing, smiling, and dancing in a seductive manner under the tarp in the middle of the yard. Weddings, wakes, and funerals tended to offer very rare moments of joy in a country, in the communities ravaged by natural hazards. In this wake, homeless and poor inhabitants were sure to have drinks, meals, and alcoholic beverages. The De Family was able to receive comfort in the midst of this general tribulation but it was at a cost of feeding the mass willing to come over.

Rose, Carline, and most of the young kids managed to find a spot inside the large living room in the midst of important adults and the rest of the family. They were all too happy to stay away from the rain and despair surrounding all the city. They knew they would not be able to stay there until nightfall. They were expecting the arrival of their parents. TiGrimo was waiting for his father to show up. However, GroGrimo was too busy working, supervising the building of coffins at Boss Manno's coffin shop. From time to time, the two girls went out to watch the women cooking in the kitchen. They were more attracted by the young women's art of seduction. But at their age and in the midst of a recent series of traumatic events caused by the hurricane and quake, they could not understand everything they were observing. It was almost too much for their small brain. Yet, it was too much overstimulation for them after walking around the city that was almost devastated by the natural disasters. The girls decided to stay away from the afternoon rain. Their family members were too busy looking for family members who were disappeared by the strong winds of the hurricane. They did not have time to watch them. Most parents did not have time to take care of the surviving kids. They had lost everything. They soon became depressed by so much loss and so much pain. They stopped forbidding their girls to go out in the rain or at night. Most mothers were suffering so much that they stopped preventing their daughters from walking in the rain which would mess up their processed hair. The girls' hair already returned to their dreaded natural state. The hurricane tended to dehumanize the survivors. They were exposed to the rest of the world. It was as if they were naked. Even Mother Nature appeared to want to inflict as much pain as possible to the body of the people of this island. These were the same people whose ancestors fought against slavery, humiliation, and a global put down of the black race. Yet, they managed to survive and beat colonial powers and capitalism built on their back.

After falling asleep on the corner of the living room while the adults were busy talking to each other, the girls got up and decided to leave the wake. They had more places to visit and observe. They wanted to continue to bear witness to the vast destruction.

"Oh my God! This is the catholic church where I was baptized," screamed TiGrimo as he invited his friends to walk up the steps of the once gorgeous church whose rooftop was blown away.

"Nothing is left. Some of the remaining benches are blown to the pulpit," said another witness who was standing next to Rose holding her sister's hand.

Some churchgoers also came to witness the devastation. Others were crying and praying. They remained on their knees for a long time. They did not care about the potholes, cracked beams, and muds caused by the broken parts of the church wall.

Carline sad down close to a woman she knew because she always stopped by her parents' house to sell some of her merchandise. She remembered her well because she sold mountain-grown carrots, watercress, goat milk, and fresh eggs. Carline heard her prayers. The mountain woman, TiMadanm Carmona, was naming the names of the deceased ones, the neighbors and farmers who were blown away by the hurricane. She had her rosary beads in her hand. Carline did not understand the importance of the prayer beads. She watched the mountain woman moving her fingers from one bead to another. She was counting the series of prayers while concentrating on the mysteries. She was reciting each individual prayer of this comforting catholic devotion.

"Mother Marie, bless the soul of the departed friends and mountain dwellers. Lord, protect the survivors of the hurricane. You have blessed and protected them up to this time. You did not let them perish during the January 12, 2010 quake," prayed the mountain merchant or Madan Sara.

Carline listened to her as she was naming the places that were attacked and ravaged by Hurricane Matthew. The mountain woman either traveled to all of these coastal cities or met with her fellow Madan Saras, (traveling merchants) in Jeremie, Les Cayes or Port-au-Prince's Markets such as Croix-des-Bossales or Iron Market.

"Re-animate the soul of the residents in the following coastal towns: Abricots, Trou Bonbon, Moron, Roseaux, Corail, Pestel, Presqu'Ile des Baradères, Petit Trou de Nippes, Dame Marie, Anse d'Hainault, Les Irois, Tiburon, Chardonnières, Les Anglais, Port-à-Piment, Camp-Perrin, Côteaux, Roch-à-Bateau, Port-Salut, Saint Jean du Sud, Île-À-Vache. I have not heard from my friends, my fellow Madan Saras, those of us who work so hard to educate our kids and feed our family," prayed TiMadanm Carmona as she recounted the prayer beads in her hand.

Carline looked at TiGrimo and Rose who were walking on the pulpit of the church. She made a few signals calling them to come to her area. She placed her finger on her lips asking them to be quiet as they arrived where she was standing and watching TiMadanm Carmona rolling her rosary beads.

The three kids became enchanted by what they were observing and listening to. All the while, the mountain woman, TiMadanm Carmona, never opened her eyes to even see the kids around her.

The kids whispered to each other's ears. And one by one, they tiptoed away from the benches. When they got to what used to be the entrance of the church, they exploded in laughter. And they ran away into the streets.

Carline, Rose, and TiGrimo walked down to the open-air market right in the middle of the town. The whole area was covered by trash, pieces of paper, woods, branches, fresh sand brought by the sea when it visited the main boulevard. TiGrimo was older than the two girls.

While all of three of them could read, TiGrimo was more attracted to the various colors and pictures that littered the fields. On two occasions, he stopped to pick up a few magazines their owners would not want kids to see. Hurricane Matthew revealed the hidden secrets of most families. Tourists and foreigners who have established in Port-Salut, Ile-A-Vache, Les Irois, Dame Marie... for years have been bringing magazines, articles, and picture books they grew up with. With the arrival of the Internet, they did not need to keep bringing them from Canada, the US, France, Germany and other countries. Using their solar panels and electricity, they were able to access their favorite websites for all kinds of news and entertainment. Yet, those tourists never got rid of their old magazines that their own parents and grandparents used to hide under their bed. They brought them to their home in Les Cayes and forgot about them over the years. Hurricane Matthew blew up their hidden secrets that were spread all over the landscape.

Chapter 4

What's Left of the Market

Three days later, the surviving residents of the nearby communities were able to meet at the open-air market. Before the hurricane, merchants used to sell their merchandise in the few market buildings surrounding the numerous stalls. Those buildings withstood many previous hurricanes, but Hurricane Matthew was a beast that focused on the destruction of the southern peninsula. It wanted to drop them to their knees. It managed to do so by destroying livestock, homes, and killing people.

Early on Saturday morning, the buses were loaded with merchants, Madan Saras, and clients. The bus drivers and their assistants traveled all the way to the surrounding mountains and hills to load the fresh fruits, vegetables, and agricultural products or crops from their field. They wanted to bring them back to the market where city dwellers.

While the bus workers were busy loading up the various bags of vegetables, the drivers had enough time to play domino, visit their friends, girlfriends, and eat breakfast at nearby shops. There were always residents who were ready to sell hot meals to bus drivers, merchants, and travelers. In the case of some drivers, over the years, they managed to become friends with the most popular peasants who instructed their domestics to prepare meals for them. Those peasants appeared to have the schedule of the bus drivers.

Maxo was the most reliable bus driver in the whole region. Most of the peasants, merchants, Madan Saras trusted him because he never had an accident in all his years of driving to almost inaccessible areas of the communities. Whenever those merchants wanted a reliable driver to transport their merchandise to bigger markets in the major cities and the capital, they called Maxo who ended up scheduling one day a week for long-distance trips. Maxo figured out that Wednesdays were the best day to transport them to the capital. The merchants will be able to sell and purchase new merchandise to take back to their village. These merchants wanted to be back on Friday so they could go to the crowded Saturday market. They expected to sell most of their merchandise.

As most of the merchants took longer to bring their merchandise to the bus loaders, Maxo checked the way his bus was being loaded with all those bags and heads of live cattle and chickens. He decided everything was going well. He relied on two of his most trusted assistants. Once he has talked to them, he decided to visit one of his best friends.

Viviana was the most popular madan Sara, merchant of the community. She had her own store which her husband, a former judge, Balthazar, built for her. She had many beautiful daughters who were studying in Port-au-Prince. Viviana used to send presents and money to them through Maxo. Viviana's girls depended on her and their father to survive in the capital. Over the years, one of them, Margo, was getting very close to Maxo who went to the same elementary school with her in their village. So it was common for Maxo to stay away from the beating sun on the front porch of the store. As Viviana relied on many of her employees to sell her products in the store, she had enough time to meet her long-time clients and friends.

Viviana sat on the long front porch of her store in one of those refurnished rocking chairs with two or three cushions underneath. On her right side, she had beautiful flowers and hibiscus plants covering the balcony. Stairways surrounded by all kinds of tropical plants led to the family's private residence on top of the store. Viviana enjoyed watching her former customers pass in front of her residence and store. If she was not reading and drinking coffee or tea on the top balcony, she was sitting on the front porch with a small table on her right side. She had a habit of serving coffee and tea to her friends and former customers. Depending on the season, she would have bread, fruits, or gingerbread cakes or cookies. The goal was she would get the most recent news about what was in season. Then, she would dispatch her buyers to the fields to purchase for the store, warehouse, or bodega.

Viviana had a few close friends who would drop by to chat with her and drink her favorite coffee and tea. Maxo was one of them. Viviana relied on him to run a few errands for her in Port-au-Prince. She also sent money and other seasonal products to her daughters studying in the capital. Most importantly, she relied on Maxo to get the latest news of the city and peasants. Viviana was in communication with most of the Madan Saras who have respected her over the years. Viviana's husband who continues to be respected all over the city by all residents despite his retirement. Judge Balthazar had a long history of advocating for the small guys. He stood up for the middle men and women, the street merchants and market women who were being coerced by the bogeymen or Tonton Macoutes. Judge Balthazar even found great respect from the bad guys because he was fair. He would take time to explain the laws to the peasants as well as the pirate city dwellers. On a few days, Judge Balthazar would take time from his reading and study room to sit with his wife on the front porch. Over the years, he had received many of his former court cases on the porch. Everybody was always very cordial to him. Whenever they would see him on the front porch, they would stop to greet him and take coffee or tea with him. Some of them would even bring him presents which he declined. But they would not leave with them any way.

"Judge Balthazar, I greet you in the name of my family. We are still on our property thanks to you," yelled an old man tying his horse to a post under the quenêpe tree in the front yard. Judge Balthazar was watering one of his best flowers in the front. He enjoyed taking care of his property despite having a gardener. It was a way for him to get up and stretch his legs from all of his reading and studying. In so doing, he was able to see and be seen by his church and court friends.

"Mr. Altidor, It's been a long time since I saw you in court. You know the way I work. As much as I could, I would not let the personal police forces of late dictators Francois and Jean Claude Duvalier throw you off your lands. They were thieves who would conduct any extortion in plain daylight," responded Judge Balthazar.

"I just wish they were judges like you these days. In our times, judges are bought. If the price is right, then you will win no matter what. Judges become politicians who are more concerned over their own profits," said Mr. Altidor.

"There are a few good judges still in this world. The bad ones make more noise. They are louder. That's all," said Balthazar.

"Yes, they are like dogs who bark over any little things because they have to defend the rich land thieves."

"What brought you to town today?" asked Judge Balthazar who invited him to take a seat on the front porch where his wife was waiting.

"I have heard my husband talking about this case when it was going on. It cost him a few nightmares, but in the end, he was very happy to render justice," said Viviana who offered a cup of coffee to Mr. Altidor.

"Tell us how things are going on in the mountains," said Viviana.

"Mrs. Balthazar, I want to thank you for taking care of such a great man. Judge Balthazar is the kind of judge this country needs. There is so much injustice right now in this country. The worst thing that is going on right now is that a lot of billionaires from other countries are coming to buy prime land. I do not know how this is happening now. What did Dessalines say in the constitution?" said Mr. Altidor.

"They are happening because one way or the other these multinationals, foreign corporations, and billionaires managed to have Bill Clinton to cause the then-president of Haiti to amend the constitution, thus allowing them and their friends to start buying the best mines, coastal lands to build hotels and other businesses. I have read that even Bill Clinton and his wife bought some land in this country," replied Judge Balthazar.

"A Republican friend of my son who is studying in the US told him that when Hillary Clinton was Secretary of State under Obama, she was able to help her brother get a rare 20-year-plus gold mine permit in Haiti. VCS Mining mines gold in Morne Bossa, Haiti. Tony Rodham, brother of Hillary Clinton, is on the VCS board. The same goes for former Haitian Prime Minister Jean-Max Bellerive who worked side by side with Bill Clinton after the 2010 quake," said Mr. Altidor.

It was only at that point that Viviana chose to intervene in the serious conversation between those two men.

"I do not know if it's true, but when Hillary Clinton was running for President of the United States, she and her husband denied it. She stated she had nothing to do with her brother being on the advisory VCS Mining board. She added that Tony is a well-known entrepreneur, businessman who has been very successful on his own. I would hope that the Haitian government would want to make sure that Haiti receives her fair share of the profits."

"Viviana, I can tell you this. You are looking here at a man, Mr. Altidor, who will never sell his land. He and his friends would rather leave them the way it has been. Once those foreigners buy your land, you will never be able to get it back. They will chase us off of our own heritage just the way they chased the Native Americans to the reservations all over this continent. The first thing is that we will not be able to enjoy our own beachfront," stated Judge Balthazar who rose up to shake hands with Mr. Altidor.

"Elections in most third-world countries can be brutal and dangerous. For the first time, I have seen how nasty presidential campaigns are in the United States. My Republican friends took me to a rally a few months ago while I was visiting my son, I almost vomited when I witnessed how Americans were treating their fellow men. Obviously, my conservative Republican friends apologized for the type of toxic and foul language they exposed me too," said Mr. Altidor.

"People from other countries were laughing at the nastiness and childishness of the presidential candidates. The more insult, the more lies, the more hatred, the more racist messages, scathing rant and smear campaign, the more foul language one can inflict on the other, the more chance one had to win the elections. Talking about policies did not matter as the majority of Americans proved it in the end. As a former judge, I can tell you this. Those candidates diminished the ideals of democracy that the USA has been able to promote all over the world," said Judge Balthazar, while pouring more coffee for his guest.

"Allow me to tell Mr. Altidor that this coffee came from Costa Rica. One of our daughters, Gisèle, spent two semesters there to study Spanish. She made friends with the children of the family she was staying with. That family grows coffee on their huge hacienda as our daughter's pictures showed. From time, she receives presents from them. Gisèle gave them to us," said Viviana.

"Oh this coffee has an earthy feeling. Its aroma is appealing. Its taste is very fruity," responded Mr. Altidor.

"I concur. It reminds me of the early days of coffee production in our country. Now going back to the elections, I like the idea of a strong candidate who promises to make the USA great again. But it should not happen on the back of the minorities, First Nations, people of color, the Dreamers, and immigrants. Human rights should be respected," said Judge Balthazar.

"Well, it's very hard for the USA because it was built on hatred. The white supremacists will want you to believe that it's their rights to do as they want," said Mr. Altidor. "Racism is still something Mexicans, Hispanics, Black people or people of color are going through every day in the USA. My son who is studying in one of the top US universities can tell you how common it is."

"I will tell you one thing. The USA has a long history of dealing with those inequalities. The Civil Rights Movement dealt with the KKKs' lynching, discrimination, overt racism, and lots of injustice. It is true that dealing with systemic racism will take time. The USA has gone from Dream to Hope. It will be hard to go back to the way things were back in the 1800s. My grandkids will be able to live in a better world."

"Judge Balthazar, you still believe in the fraternity of human kind. When my son returns next summer, I will tell him to visit you. This way, he can give you an update on the way life is in the states. But I can tell you that when he feels depressed by all the street shootings, the killings of innocent people in the major cities, he sometimes finds fellow Americans who give him hope. In other words, there are still good Americans," said Mr. Altidor.

"What makes you feel different from your son's belief? Asked Viviana.

"Well, I have seen many NGOs that come to this country after the 2010 quake. They are more concerned over the business of poverty than the suffering Haitian men and women. Some NGOs collect funds even when they do not have anybody in the field. They are blood suckers who are living on the back of victims. Whether it was the 2010 quake or Hurricane Matthew, the most important thing for those NGOs is the money that comes from the business of disaster," replied Mr. Altidor.

"From the Gouverneur, the Clinton Family known in Haiti as 'The King and Queen of Haiti' to the local administration and president of Haiti, there is some blame to spread everywhere. People were living on the streets, under tarps for months and years. The money that was pledged for the rebuilding of Haiti was not spent for the suffering people. How many homes did the American Red Cross build?" asked Judge Balthazar.

"This is where Haiti suffered another catastrophic disaster. The pain of the suffering Haitians was not alleviated by the building of homes. Red Cross only built 6 new permanent homes in Haiti with all that money. Yes, after raising half a billion dollars for Haiti, only 6 homes were built!" exclaimed Mr. Altidor. "Nothing else. How can thousands of people rendered homeless by the earthquake find housing in 6 homes? That was sad. How about the location of the new Manufacturing Park? Caracol is in the North of Haiti. No quake hit Cap-Haitien! Why could it not be built where the quake hit? People needed to work to be able to rebuild," said Mr. Altidor.

"It all depends on who was deciding, planning the construction of this park whose goal has been to make garments to send to the USA. Just ask Max and Bill!" replied Judge Balthazar.

As soon as Mr. Altidor finished drinking his cup of coffee, he bid farewell to the Viviana and her husband. He had to meet with his party.

Judge Balthazar walked up to his office. He stopped on the balcony to check his plants. Viviana remained seated on the porch. She hoped to have more friends who will drop by to give her their news updates.

By then, it was time for Maxo to leave. He made sure to talk to Viviana before driving her clients to the market.

"Viviana, I will drive a load to Port-au-Prince tomorrow morning. Do you have anything to send to the girls?" Maxo asked.

"Let me find out." Viviana called Marinette, one of her domestics. "What did Gisèle want from us? You told me she wanted to get a few things for this weekend party."

Marinette went to the back office to check her notes. She picked up a small bag on the corner. She took it to Viviana who handed it to Maxo.

"Please tell Gisèle that her goddaughter, her sister and their parents survived Hurricane Matthew. They were seen walking all over the communities to check their friends, but they have not been seen since then."

"I will tell them. Will you participate in the village feast this evening?" asked Maxo.

"My husband and I will go. We can't miss it. Maybe we will hear different stories about what has been happening around here. I will tell you when you get back Saturday."

"My family will go to a few funerals this tomorrow. So many people died that they had to select which funerals to attend," said Maxo.

"Judge Balthazar asked me to accompany him to two funerals tomorrow afternoon. He wants to pay his respect to the families of some of the best court workers he has ever worked with. The deceased were loyal workers who fought for the peasants, Madan Saras or Saras, and families under the two dictatorial regimes of the Duvalier," Viviana said.

Maxo left with the small bag. He placed it right behind him to make sure he did not misplace it.

Viviana called one of the warehouse workers. She wanted to go over the list of products. She did not want the warehouse to go without. In this case, she was preparing her next trip to the capital where she often bought wholesale merchandise. The warehouse employee made a final check by inspecting all the bags in the depot. She was surprised by the cat whose eyes she saw before turning on the light. She had better gotten it done right away because blackout was very common in those days. The cat jumped to another corner of the room and hid behind other bags of rice. Thanks to that cat, the mice have not been able to destroy the warehouse's products.

Viviana took advantage of the electricity by turning on her fan on the front porch. She has survived 60 summers on this island. However, she has not been able to adapt to the hellish heat in August and September. In some years, the heat wave continued all the way to October. The only temporary relief arrived with the passing of hurricanes that left more trouble with flooding and loss of livestock and human lives.

Viviana knew that she could rely on the breeze from the ocean in the evenings, but it was not every night. That's why her husband, Judge Balthazar and she found refuge on the second story veranda at night. After releasing their German shepherds and other Haitian dogs, they were able to fall asleep with the light breeze coming from the ocean.

Otherwise, they did not have to worry about burglary and lootings. They often complained about blackout in the city. But they also had to worry about shootings and lootings provoked by protestors paid by business competitors. One thing that Viviana knew was that good relationship could always trump hatred and violence. By feeding the poor and helping pay the education of their children, she was respected and protected by most residents. Her own daughters baptized some of those kids. She considered them as family members. Viviana knew that she was privileged and had a responsibility to help her people. On the front porch of her family business, she made time to talk to everybody. She also made sure she had enough coffee or tea for the day. So many children came to know her as the town's benefactor. When they came, she asked them about their parents, how they were doing in school, what was their favorite subject. She promised to give the girls a present if they maintained good grades. The most important thing for her was whether those boys and girls were reading. And she was very happy to listen to their stories on the front porch.

Shy girls became extrovert. They were ready to embrace the world and all it had to offer to them. Viviana remembered the women in her own life when she was growing up. She respected her mother's educated friends as well as her servants or domestics who took care of the household needs. When it was her time to tell her own stories, the kids either her own girls or husband baptized were happy to listen to her. And she told them her favorite stories about Madan Saras or Saras. She was talking to kids whose mothers were Saras. By the way, Viviana told her stories, those kids got to appreciate their mothers' business. They knew they were the main breadwinners of the family.

It was Viviana's turn to tell her young visitors another story.

"Who would say that I would be where I am right now? My parents did not have a lot of money when they were children like you. Their parents had to work in the field. The only difference was that their own parents – My grandparents- had lots of land. And they found people who

wanted to work for them. They paid them well enough that they never stopped working for them. My mother, Mrs. De, told me that she learned at an early age that buying cheap and selling at a markup will bring money to the family. She started selling with her own mom and aunts. By the time she was 14, she was selling for her grandfather, father, and other people. She knew how to talk to the farmers who trusted her. They also knew that she needed a few strong men to accompany her to the market. So they sent her to the market with the most fearsome employee who loaded up the donkeys, mules, and horses. During that time, those animals were the safest and only transportation modes they had. That's way before the buses and taptaps arrived. One of my favorite things was to accompany my mother in the market on Saturdays. If I was not in school, I would be with her in the market. Even when I was in school during the week, I'd go to the market to learn from her. I watched how Mrs. De talked to her clients, how she displayed and offered her merchandise to them. She always had two small benches in her stall for her customers. While she waited for the next customers to buy her products, she could learn so much from the others who came from other communities and nearby islands. She would get up to measure the rice, beans, and other products. She would always make sure she added a small portion for the customer's children whose stories she knew by now. She always made sure to ask her clients about their family, kids, church activities, and fields. Mrs. De wanted to know what they were growing because she could sell for them too. That could be another source of profit for her. After earning enough money, she became a full-fledged Madan Sara who traveled and connected growers with buyers. She went to hard-to-reach villages to buy the fresh produce from peasants, farmers despite the personal risk to herself on the roads. I remember that my mother had to let her donkey go alone ahead of her one night because she was returning from a nearby town. In those days, people were being kidnapped by the regime's bogeymen to keep them in captivity in order to get their blood to sell to foreign blood banks. Mrs. De found out about those things from her past friends who disappeared and never were seen in the market again. So alone on the road, she saw the light of a suspicious car around the corner of the road, she threw her bag, jumped off the saddle of the donkey, and let her eat grass along the way. She ran into a nearby plantain field where she hid until the car left. From her refuge, she could see that the driver stopped the car. A few men started looking around with a flash light. As they were approaching the donkey, she turned around to glare at them, started to bray loudly, proceeded to aggressively attack them. When they observed the donkey's move, they backed away, they did not want to get caught by her owner. Donkey thieves were shot right on the scene in those days. By then, it was getting very late. Having not seen her at home, my grandfather, accompanied by some of his fiercest workers and other neighborhood strongmen, launched a search party for Mrs. De. In those days, her name was Tizwit, a name given to skinny little girls. Along the way, my grandfather and their men, accompanied by 4 of the most vicious dogs he had on his property, were calling, 'Tizwit, where are you? Has anybody seen Tizwit passing by on a gray donkey? Hello Tizwit, if you are around, if you are hiding somewhere, come out.' My grandfather and the search party were saying amidst the barking of the dogs. Needless to say more people started to join the search party. They started to walk with them and support them along the way. Strangers heard the dogs' barking and the voice of the search men. They also reported to my grandfather that a suspicious car had been spotted around the corner a few nights ago. They informed her that one night the driver and passengers made a catch that did not go well. Those kidnappers or blood suckers ran into the wrong guys. It was the night Baron Samedi or Baron Lacroix, Grandmother Brigitte and Papa Gede were out on their ritual neighborhood promenade. Just so you know, the neighbors watched as they approached Baron Samedi, caught him and tried to force him into their world-war II Jeep. They did not know that the elegantly dressed, black top-hatted dapper sapeur was the very voodoo divinity providing over the cemetery, death, birth, sex, and rebirth. In less than two minutes, the man who claimed to be an immaterial being was accompanied by his hooded men, thugs, prone to commit violence at the drop of his hat. Baron Samedi transformed and got out of the vehicle to the amazement of the human traffickers who tried to leave but they were arrested by the hooded Tonton Macoutes. Soon thereafter the search party saw the donkey eating grass along the way. She recognized Tizwit's father who rushed to control her to prevent her from running away. But she knew those dogs too. It was only at that point that Tizwit came out of her plantain field where she was hiding. All the men and dogs approached Tizwit. 'Are you ok,' they asked her. After answering that she got scared by the car that was parked around the corner, she got into the saddle on the donkey. The whole search party returned to their home. One by one, the volunteers were bidding her farewell and told her to ask them for help the next time she needed a walking companion. Since most of them had young daughters who were Tizwit's age, they saw her as a role model for them. She joined the Madan Sara club at a young age. From that day on, Tizwit's parents –my grandparents- did not let her go too far away without any personal assistants. Preventing a young Madan Sara from traveling to the far-away communities to purchase merchandise would not be easy, especially if profits can be made."

Viviana had her young visitors' attention wrapped around her finger. She was a great storyteller. She sent them to her employees to get either a piece of dous makos, gingerbread or soursop juice. Depending on the fruits of the season her peasant or Madan Sara friends brought to her, Viviana's young visitors would enjoy special mangos, fresh organic bananas, and coconut juice. Viviana's employees appeared to have a special way of making sweetsop, sugar apple or custard apple juice attracting the kids to Viviana's story time on the porch. Viviana learned so much from Mrs. De, her mother. She always wanted to give back to her community's children. Storytime with Viviana on the porch started one summer when she saw a lot of kids were coming over to play with her girls who used to read to them. But after they left the village to study in the capital, Viviana did not want such a great activity to stop. She took over the 2-hour storytelling sessions. And the kids enjoyed coming over to listen to her beautiful stories. More importantly, they were attracted by the various treats.

Over the years, Viviana learned the names of most of those kids. Their parents always preferred them to be with Viviana for two hours instead of playing in the ocean where many of them could drown. Every week, the kids had one hour to tell her their own stories. And Viviana used the rest of the time to tell them her own stories. Before leaving her, they knew they would get their seasonal treat.

Right after the quake, Viviana started missing some of the kids who used to come to her storytelling sessions. The January 12, 2010 quake killed and moved Viviana's friends, neighbors, and clients around. A lot of them were killed. The survivors of the quake did not have anything to live for. Life before the quake was very hard. After the quake, the hardship for most residents was unbearable. One thing that Viviana wanted to do was to remain in contact with her storytelling kids. The difference was that she could not get in touch with them.

Viviana wanted to know what happened to the two sisters, Rose and Carline. She wanted to send good news to her daughter, Gisèle. She waited for any news every day on the front porch. The last news she got was that those two girls were walking around with a boy whose father was working in the coffin shop. TiGrimo was GroGrimo's son. So Viviana asked one of her Madan Sara friends to drop by the shop to talk to GroGrimo and enquire about those two girls. Viviana was very close to Gigi and Mrs. De. Those two Madan Saras usually ran errands for her warehouse when she could not go to Port-au-Prince. So the day, Gigi showed up at the coffin shop, GroGrimo was not present. She managed to have a few words with the owner of the shop. Boss Manno should have been able to give Gigi some news. After all, everybody knew he had been making coffins for him ever since the quake. And when Hurricane Matthew hit southwestern Haiti near Les Anglais on October 4, 2016, most residents did not have anything to hold them to the land.

"Hello Boss Manno, how are you doing?" said Gigi.

"Hello Gigi, what brought you here so early?" asked Boss Manno.

"Well, I just wanted to check on my clients who have survived this horrible hurricane."

"Well, you know that's the way it is in this country. After the quake in 2010, we were not given enough time to breathe. This hurricane surprised me. It plucked all it can take out of the face of the earth."

"I know food will be scarce. Most of my farmers and peasant friends lost their livestock and agricultural crops. They did not have time to harvest them. This hurricane did not give any warning."

"That's right. But you have really told me what brought you here so early," said Boss Manno. "You can see I have been making coffins. And they have been selling very well. I have some gravediggers I befriended. They referred the family members to me."

"The main reason I come here is to find out whether you know what happened to GroGrimo," said Gigi.

"For two weeks, after the passage of hurricane Matthew, he was working here with me. He was my right arm man. We have been great buddies. But he told me he was not happy. He wanted to make a move."

"Did he tell you where he was going?" asked Gigi.

"Did you guys have a relationship? He did not tell me about that kind of relationship. He told me after the quake in 2010, he fed his family thanks to some great friends, Madan Saras. But he never named any names."

"Oh no. He was my client. I sold him a mixture of my products, such as foodstuff, household items and clothing. By clothing, I mean Pèpè. He had children he had to feed and clothe. I sell everything as long as I am able to make a penny. I treated all of my clients with respect. Over the years, we had a vendor/client relationship. Nothing else," clarified Gigi.

"Well, I understand. My wife told me that you have been selling her a lot of your merchandise. I work for my wife and kids. All she does is to spend, feed the kids and me."

"You have a good wife. She is one of my best clients. You have a great family," commented Gigi.

"Well, this has been a secret. But I am wondering whether you can keep a secret. GroGrimo is a discreet man. He did not want to tell anybody what he was up to."

"Where is he? You said he wanted to make a move. What did you mean by that?"

"Well, he wanted to make more money for his family. He wanted to leave the country. He and his family were granted a visa by the Brazilian embassy. So with the money he earned from my shop, he was able to take his family to Brazil."

"Wow, how long ago? Well, why Brazil?"

"He tried to get a visa to go to Canada and the United States, but he could not get one. The door started opening when his brother and his family were granted a visa to go Brazil. His younger brother obtained a visa to go to Chile. I guess he was stung by the travel bug. In addition, he could not find another job since he lost his job at Haiti Teleco."

"It was very difficult for somebody like him who used to make decent money, had a monthly paycheck to take care of his family. Then, all of a sudden, the company goes down or is bought by other bigshots. He explained all of this to me. I had pity for him and his family."

"Please do not tell your Madan Sara friends about his business. As I said, he is a discreet man who was suffering tremendously. A former Teleco employee who was reduced to two things: to protest by burning tires or apply *Pè Lebrun* for a paycheck or make coffins for a living."

"People like GroGrimo may not be able to take it well. He had a conscience. He was dealing with unconscious administrators and employers. That's why I told him to find something he could do well.

He could become a middle-man, an entrepreneur or whatever. He is an intelligent engineer," said Gigi Madan Sara.

"Well, GroGrimo saw all the kickbacks that were taking place. He knew Haiti Teleco was being looted by the higher ups or people with lots of power. He could not let that much extortion go without being checked. Haiti Teleco was one of the sources of hard currency for the country. People use it a main utility. He was let go years before the quake. He was doing odd jobs here and there. After the quake, I brought him to my company. There is a huge need for coffins in this country. I thought he would stay with me for many years. But he was stung by the travel bug," said Boss Manno.

"How can one function in a place with no transparency? He could not go public because he wanted a job. He had several mouths to feed. So he was shocked by his firing. Boss Manno, I thought he was going to stay at your coffin shop for a long time."

"GroGrimo was telling me that each nail he placed on a coffin was like a nail he was placing on his future. He needed to go away. He needed to breathe. He told me those things because we grew up together. We talked after work was over. I even baptized one of his kids. TiGrimo is my godson."

"I am sorry to see your pain. You seem to have lost a good friend."

"Yes, I felt so sorry that someone so intelligent, so educated had to leave the country. It's what they call brain drain."

"Have you been able to talk to him since his departure?"

"Yes, I had to call him on a few occasions. I sent a few presents to my godson. I was close to all of his family members. It looks like things did not pan out in Brazil. He told me that Brazil wanted braceros to get ready for the Olympic Games. They had a lot building projects. Haitians are being piled like sardines in a box. Then, when the Brazilian economy had a nosedive, most Haitians were ready to go to the North. He told me that his next move would be to go to the US."

"What a life? Haitians become the Jews of the Old Testament. They become parts of the huge global migration wave."

"Is there anything else you want to know? I have a few customers who have just arrived here. They want to talk to me about a few coffins. I have to talk to my employees and those clients," said Boss Manno.

"Yes, thank you for your time. Before leaving, do you know anything about two girls named Carline and

Rose?"

"GroGrimo told me that the last time she saw them and their parents, they were in a crowded shelter in

Brazil. They were making plans to travel to the North with another group of Haitians, Asians, and

Central Americans," Boss Manno said.

Gigi Madan Sara bid farewell to Boss Manno. She returned to her home, took a bath, ate dinner before

heading to the afternoon funeral. She did not want to miss one of her fellow Madan Sara's funerals.

Gigi belonged to this tight network of female entrepreneurs in a country and culture that did not give

them any other options. She knew she had to pay her last respect to her commère, her road

companion. Gigi knew she would run into Viviana and her husband at this funeral. She would make sure to accompany them to their home located a few blocks away from hers.

Chapter 5

Brain Drain: The Desperate Trek to the North

Survivors of January 12, 2010 Quake and October 4, 2016 Hurricane Matthew Started their Journey to the North

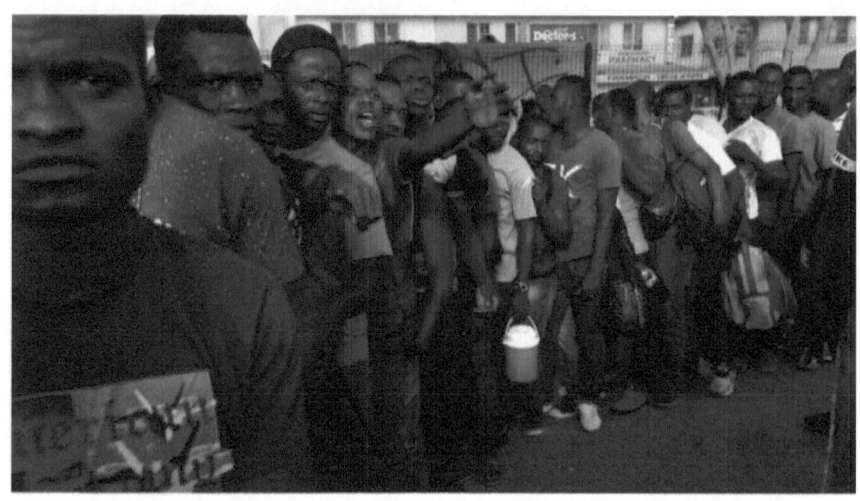

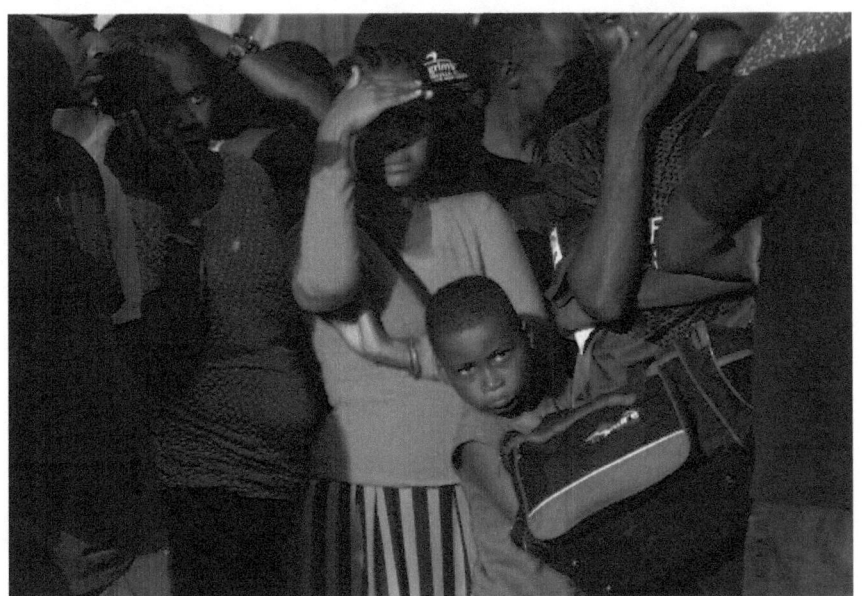

The January 12, 2010 quake killed thousands of Haitians. The survivors of the quake became homeless. Haiti's capital and nearby towns became the epicenter of the new Tarp or Tent Nation. While the International community pledged to help rebuild the country, many Haitians knew the pledged aid would not get to the poor survivors. They were ready to leave the country. They had no home to go back to. And they did not have any means to rebuild them. So most Haitians were trying to find a visa to any foreign country. The neighboring Caribbean countries received any Haitian emigrants. 6 years later, Hurricane Matthew destroyed the southwestern part of Haiti. The landfall was in Les Anglais.

More and more Haitians suffered from these natural disasters. Haitians were traveling to RD, Chile, Bahamas or any other country willing to welcome them. As Brazil was getting ready to hold the Olympic Games, it needed builders. Many Haitians ended up going to Brazil with the hope of finding decent work so they could help their family members left behind. Once the games were over, around the same time, Brazilian economy tanked. Once more, Haitian migrants decided to leave Brazil when they started losing their meagre work. In a tough economy, there was a battle for employment. Unable to work and live in non-crime ridden communities, they decided to take the trek to the North. However, they did not know how long the journey would be and whether they would survive along the way.

Gigi Madan Sara sat on Viviana's front porch. As usual, Viviana called one of her domestics to bring a cup of coffee for her favorite guest. In the meantime, she started conversing with Gigi. Viviana wanted to get her updates.

"Tell me what you were able to find out. Did you go to Boss Manno's coffin shop?"

"Yes. I received good news for you. It looks like the girls are still alive."

"Where are they? How come I have not seen them here? They used to come to my storytelling sessions," said Viviana, excited to find out what happened to them.

"Well, you may not see Carline, Rose and their family members for a while."

"Did they move to another city?"

"No. According to Boss Manno, Brazil granted a visa to their family. So, the girls' father took his family to live with his brother. Boss Manno said that things did not work out for them. The brother was still living in a shelter. And he had already decided to travel to the US/ Mexican border."

"It's a major problem for all of these people who are trying to make it to the US before the next president takes office on January 20, 2017."

"I never thought about it this way. I have not been paying attention to the news. My radio needed new batteries."

"Well, you can come here to listen to the news with me. Based on what I heard during the long presidential campaign in the US, one of the candidates plans on building a wall. It looks like most countries that used to welcome Haitians are saying no to them now. For almost a year and a half, there has been such a huge drama in DR. Dominicans of Haitian descent are being called names and abused. They are sending them back to Haiti. Most of these people do not know anything but DR."

"Well, I will buy a few batteries for the radio before I get back home tonight. My kids enjoy listening to the news too."

"You'd better do this. One way or the other, we may know somebody who is part of this adventure," said Viviana.

"When Madan Sara buddies start leaving the country in wave, then we know that we have a major problem in this country."

"I agree with you. My husband and I have been talking about this problem for a long time. Gigi, you are telling the truth."

"According to what Boss Manno told me, more than half of the young men from the nearby communities have already left for Ecuador on their way to Brazil. Since 2011, 2012, 2013 and on, men, women, and children have been on this desperate trek. If GroGrimo wanted to travel, he had many reasons to not stay. He had family members who had already made the trip."

While Viviana and Gigi were talking, Maxo arrived with his news from the capital. He hugged both women on the front porch. He quickly said that Viviana's daughters sent their greetings. Then, as if he was at home, he went straight to the shower in the back. Coming from a long day of driving from Croix des Bossales in Port-au-Prince and Croix des Bouquets, he was not only tired but he was also hungry. He knew he would find enough water to clean himself at Viviana's residence despite the occasional lack of running water from the local water company.

Down on the street in the front of her house were two mountain women on the back of their mules. On their left side stood 4 business women who were carrying loads of fresh fruits on their head. They were talking to each other. They made sure to stop in front of Viviana's warehouse to offer their products to her. On many occasions, they only wanted her to know what they were going to display in the open-air market. This way, Viviana could quickly dispatch one of workers to run errands. Those street merchants knew how to treat their 'good pratik, good customers.' They reserved the best merchandise for them.

All of a sudden, a bus heading to the nearby market stopped in front of Viviana's front porch. Viviana knew who was coming to greet her. Christel and Viviana remained good friends over the years. In the last few years, Christèle had been able to engage in the wholesaling of used clothes from overseas. She was able to travel to many foreign countries to purchase Pèpè, used or secondhand clothes in huge amounts. She was doing so well that she managed to purchase her own truck to sell used clothes in various markets. She sold mostly in the capital or in major provinces such as Cap-Haitien, Gonaïves, Croix-des-Bouquets etc. She stopped by Viviana's house to chat with her on her way to the local beach where her parents still lived.

"Viviana, how beautiful you remain! Nothing changed in you. You remain the same person. You have to give me the secret," said Christèle, hugging and kissing Viviana on both sides of her face.

"I did not think you would stop to see me. You have been too busy making money and traveling. Last month, I was told you came to town, but you did not care about seeing me."

"It was a quick stop to say hi to my parents. I had some business deals in Cavaillon, Miragoâne, Léogâne, Petit-Goâve and Grand-Goâve. I was too tired that day. I had to go back to P-au-Prince to receive some of my new shipments from Miami," said Christèle.

"You could have stopped her to share a cup of coffee or tea with me. I would understand you had to go in a hurry," added Viviana, looking at her best adolescent friend.

These women grew up together and went to the same local parochial school. For a long time, they wanted to become nuns. Christèle remembered Gigi Madan Sara. They would run into each other at Croix-des-Bossales, in Port-au-Prince. It was the hay day of late President Francois Duvalier also known as 'Papa Doc.' In those days, Croix-des-Bossales was clean. Madan Saras did not fear for their security as thieves and pick-pockets were shot right on the scene by undercover police officers and hooded Tonton Macoutes. Safety and security were also promoted by Jean-Claude Duvalier or Baby Doc. The VSNs or Volunteers of the National Security could do anything they wanted without any impunity. Justice was rendered right away. The business women would often meet at Iron Market and other important markets all around the capital. In those days, Gigi and Christèle competed against each other, but they learned to respect each other too.

"How about you, Gigi? Ki jan ou ye? Ki jan pitit ou yo ye? How are your kids? How have you been doing?" asked Christèle. "How is your business?"

"Well, it could have been better. The kids are all grownups now. The good days are gone. With lack of security, Madan Saras cannot make any money."

Viviana intervened and asked Christèle what she wanted to drink. She then called her husband to come down. She instructed her domestics to prepare lunch so Judge Balthazar could have lunch with Gigi, Christèle, and Maxo.

"Before my husband comes down from his study room, tell me about your husband and your son?" Viviana asked Christèle.

"My son is doing very well. You forgot to ask me about my young daughter. She is 15 years old. Both of them are attending school in Miami. After a while, I could not handle the drive-by-shootings and political upheaval here. Since I was in and out of the country, I had to send them to school in Miami."

"I understand, but you have not told me about your husband. How come he is not here with you?"

"To make a long story short, he was too jealous. He did not want to get into the business of buying and selling second-hand clothes with me. He kept saying he had his prestige. So I needed security and safety. He is the father of my children, but he let his pride and prestige take over survival in this global market."

"How come you have never told me about the divorce?"

"Well, we were separated for a long time. I wanted to make the marriage work, but he was not willing to work it out. I gave him an ultimatum. After 4 years of separation, it was time to move on. That was after the quake when my kids and I were granted a visa to travel to Chile. When I was in Chile with the kids, he called us to inform us that he obtained a visa to go work in Brazil. That's what he wanted to do any way. He is a huge fan of Brazilian football."

"Well, no wonder I have not heard from you for a few years!" said Gigi, shaking her head in support of Christèle's final decision.

"Well, I was still hoping that he would reunite with us somewhere in Brazil or Chile for the sake of the kids!" added Christèle.

"Well, God will take care of you. He never abandons his children!" sighed Viviana. "What do men want? Here is a beautiful woman, a hard-working woman who wanted to work things out with her baby father, but he decided otherwise!"

All three women remained silent. They sighed and shook their head. They all recognized how life can be difficult in the search for a good life.

"How was life in Chile?" asked Gigi.

"Well, it was not easy the first three years. The kids adapted to the language and culture quickly, but it took me some time even though I used to cross the border to do business in Dominican Republic when relationship was good."

"Was it easy to find employment, housing, and a good school for the kids?"

"Well, I was lucky enough to have had some contact with somebody who was a driver for the Chilean embassy in Haiti. I inquired about the type of visa I could get. He found out for me that being granted a work visa would be good for two years. That means I would be able to work to support my kids and my family back home. I told the Chilean consul that I could work in the hotel, food, cleaning industries."

"How long did it take you to find a job in Chile? In which field were you working?" asked Gigi.

"Chile is a very organized country. In less than a month, I was able to work in a fruit packaging company. I earned enough money that I was able to help my parents and siblings back home. I was able to take care of my family. Then, I started hearing that I could make way more money in Brazil. So I ended up leaving Chile for Brazil around the time that the Olympic Games building boom started."

"Why did you have to leave a good job like that so soon?" asked Gigi.

"Well, with the money I earned in Chile, I wanted to invest in cooking Haitian meals for sale in Brazil. Haitian workers have to eat. They would prefer to eat their own meals," I said to myself.

"Are there a lot of Haitians in Chile? Did you leave because of the competition? Or was it because of the discrimination?" asked Christèle.

"Well, It was due to both. I must say that those things did not affect me that much. I witnessed other people complaining because of the promotion they did not get. There is a lot of nativism in Chile. The Haitian immigrants did not get the best job or the promotion because Chileans needed it too. Well, guess whom the manager was going to select?"

Viviana checked with the domestics to find out whether the meals were ready. One of them came out to set the table on the front porch. She brought the dishes, spoons, forks, and a cover to prevent flies from getting to the plates. Maxo came out after taking a nap in one of Viviana's daughters' bedroom. Everybody knew that he was in a relationship with one of her beautiful daughters. The domestics knew about it. And so did Viviana who never said anything to Judge Balthazar. Nobody knew whether they were still talking. However, Maxo gets to visit all three girls in Port-au-Prince from time to time. He gave them the presents sent by Viviana.

As the table was set, Judge Balthazar made his way down from his study room. He walked towards the balcony to take a look at the blooming mango trees surrounding his home. The bees were flying in and out of the trees. The aroma of the flowers and honey could be felt far away. Judge Balthazar was not in a hurry. After all, all day long, he had his special bread, treats, and coffee in his room. But it was lunch time. It was time to eat with two guests of his wife. He did not want to upset Viviana who always made sure she made time for his own guests.

The three ladies took their seat around the table. They continued to chat and ask questions. Maxo joined them, introduced himself to Christèle and Gigi. He sat down and paid attention to the conversation.

"Christèle, you have not told us whether you have met somebody else. Do you have a boyfriend?"

"Well, when I was in Chile, I went out with a few fellow Haitians. I also met some Chileans, Bolivians, Columbians, Cubans, and Brazilians there. Actually, I could have gone out with a bunch of guys. I realized that they only wanted one thing. I was more interested in working and saving my earnings," Christèle answered.

Finally, Judge Balthazar made his way down to the table. His wife, Viviana, introduced him to Christèle. Judge Balthazar knew Gigi and Maxo who were habitual guests and friends of the family.

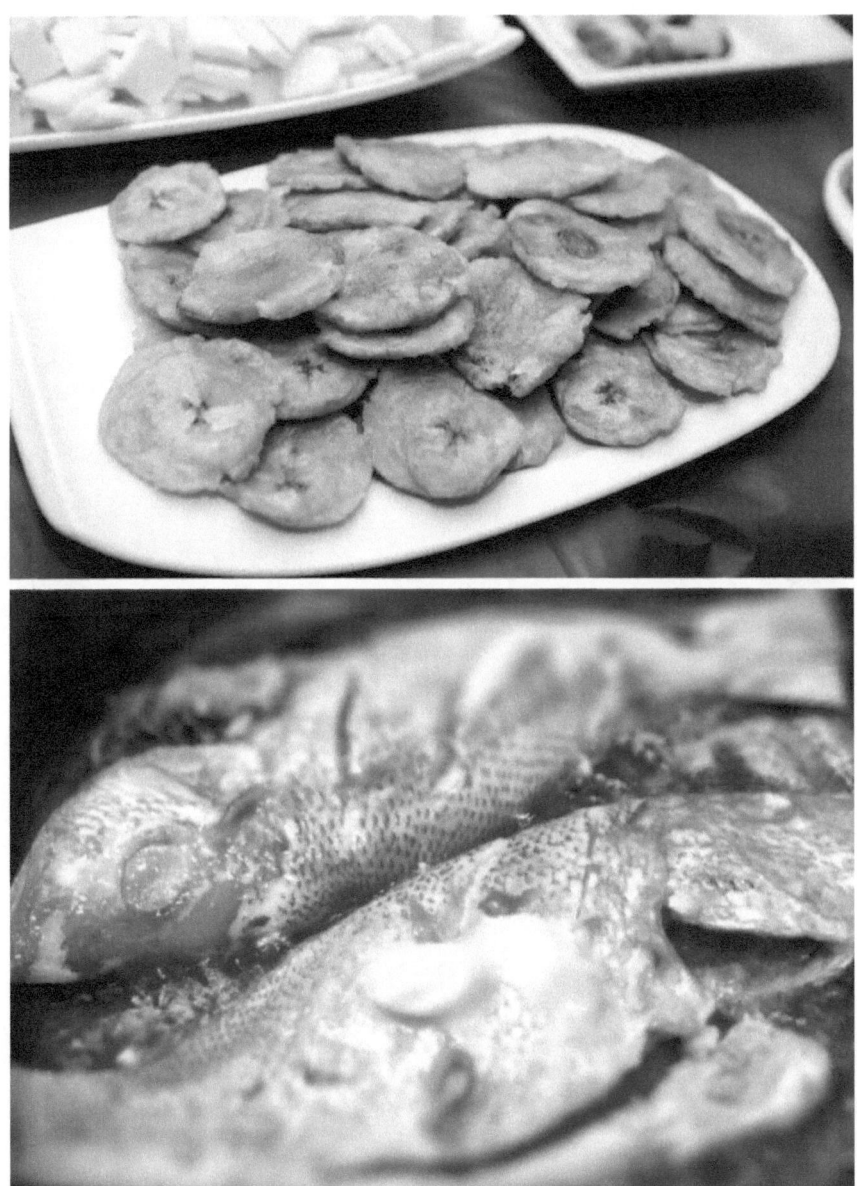

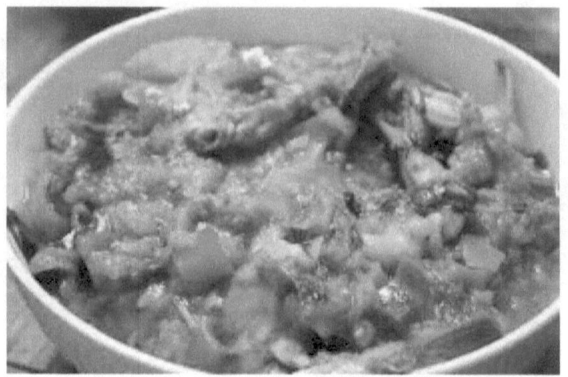

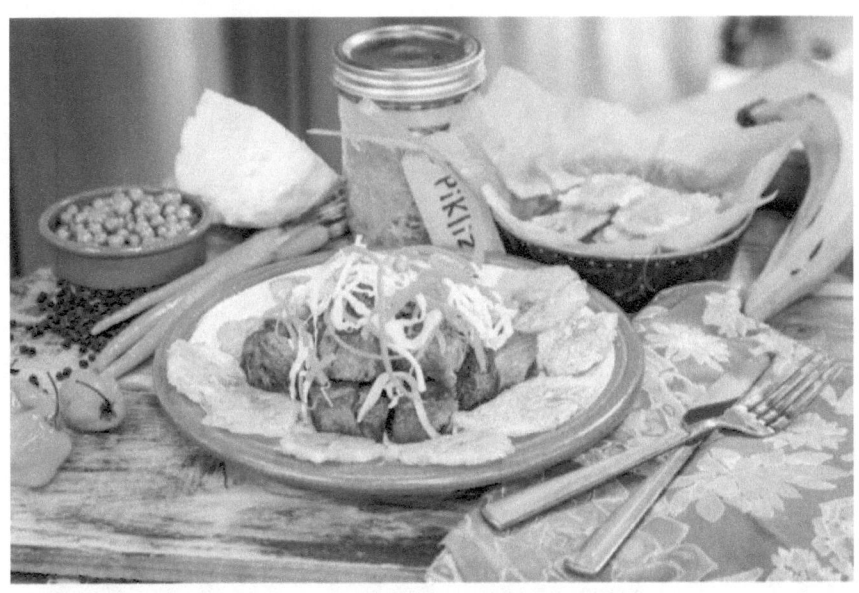

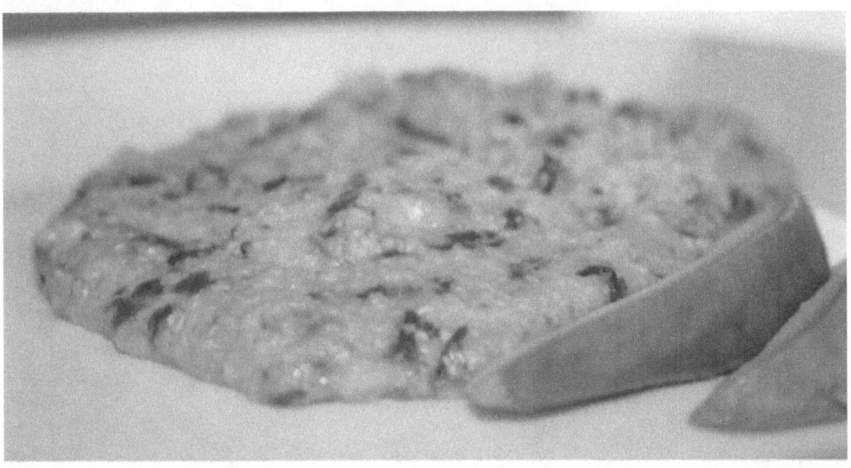

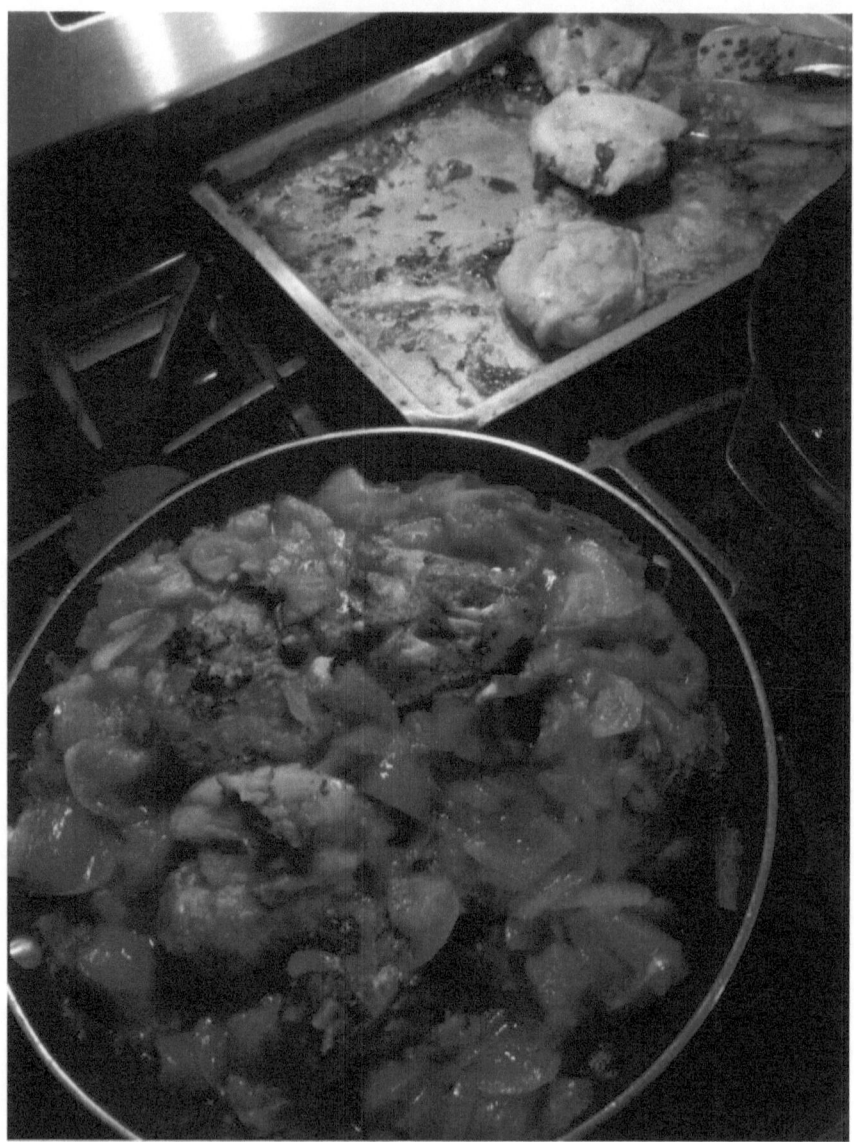

"Hello everybody. I could not come down quick enough to be with you. I was busy working on a project up there," Judge Balthazar said with a great smile.

Viviana looked at her husband and asked him whether he knew everybody around the table.

"Well, there is one person I am not too familiar with," he replied, looking at Christèle.

"This is my childhood friend, Christèle. She is a bigshot now. She has returned from Chile and Brazil where she started a business. Since then, she decided to get into the Secondhand or Used Clothes Trade."

Looking at the new face around the table, Judge Balthazar shook hands with her.

"Hello Christèle. My wife used to talk about you a lot. She told me you grew up together. It's now that I am reconnecting with some of her friends. I have just retired from the court. So now, I have time to talk and know people," Judge Balthazar said.

"Happy to be here with you. I have seen you before but you were a busy judge. I can understand you had so many cases to deal with. No problem," Christèle said politely.

"Now that the food is ready, let's say a few words of prayer. We live in a catholic country. We pray before eating," Judge Balthazar said jokingly.

Maxo finally said a few words, "We have to bless the spirits first. Haiti's a 90 % voodoo country."

Everybody laughed as he dropped some of his custard apple juice on the front porch.

"Ok, Maxo, do not bring the ants to my front porch," Viviana said jokingly.

"The spirits of our ancestors traveled in the shape of ants to watch us at any moment and anywhere," added Maxo.

"Talking about Voodoo, are the Haitians practicing voodoo in Chile and Brazil?" asked Gigi.

"Wherever Haitians go, they take their loas or spirits with them. For sure, there are few voodoo temples in Chile. In Brazil, you find Candomble which is a form of Vodou/voodoo. I ended up cooking Haitian meals for Haitian workers in Recife, Salvador de Bahia and

Rio de Janeiro. That's how I made my money. Yes, Haitians continue to celebrate their Vodou spirits," Christèle replied.

It was at that moment that Judge Balthazar decided to share his huge knowledge with his guests.

"It's an Afro-Brazilian religion. All over the Americas, you will find descendants of African slaves. So they brought their religion with them. In most Hispanic countries, there were African slaves. So the religion exists there. Whether they call it Santería in South or Central Americas, Voodoo in Louisiana, Vodou, in Haiti or Vudú in Cuba etc.

"I have also met some Mexicans who told me about curanderia. They said it's like a healer, a shaman, a type of witch doctor," said Maxo.

Everybody was enjoying the lunch prepared by Viviana's best cook. There were laughter and much joy. However, there was despair too. In his many years of being a judge in the country, Judge Balthazar never saw the amount of despair of his fellow men and women. He realized that poverty and a long history of mismanagement and unaccountability led to the current crisis Haiti is going through.

"I have fought to protect the little guys all throughout my career. I have worked hard to protect Madan Saras, street vendors who were neglected by our government and the bourgeoisie. I was one of the few judges who did not let Madan Saras get extorted and pushed out of the market by rich city dwellers and hooded men. When I see that the cornerstone, the pillar (la pierre angulaire, le pilier) of the haitian economy are leaving in mass, I am threatened. That is a cause for fear," said Judge Balthazar as he was ready to share a bottle of his favorite Cuban rum, Havana Club, with his guests. He has a long history of hosting Cuban doctors, nurses, and healthcare professionals in his home. Over the years, they brought him bottles of Havana Club.

As the guests were enjoying their meals, they never stopped asking Christèle questions. It looks like everyone was leaned on her experience as the current 'Queen Bee of the Haitian Market.' As she stated, nothing was easy. She knew how to work hard and save her money.

"Frankly, Christèle, Viviana, and Gigi, you are the types of businesspersons that this country cannot afford to lose. If all of you leave without any plan of bringing back your knowledge to the country, then we can all Haiti goodbye. She will continue to slow down farther on the global marketplace," said Judge Balthazar.

"I concur," said Maxo as he reached out for another glass of rum. By then, he was on his 4th trial. He did not know when to stop drinking.

"All those market women need is a small startup capital. Unlike the men who are more interested in buying brand shoes and high-priced fashion clothes instead of feeding and educating their children, the Haitian women will sacrifice and put their children or the family first. That's what my ex could not understand," Christèle said. After a few cups of Cuban rum, she was ready to say more than she would otherwise share. She could tell Viviana, but not everyone who was around the table.

"What would you say to Haitians who are thinking about going to Chile?" asked Maxo.

"Well, first thing first, have a work visa from a Chilean company. If you can get a work visa, you will be fine for two years, at least. I visited a workplace called, Lo Valledor. The job is to load and unload trucks. It's a vegetable and fruit company. Lots of Haitians are working there," Christèle answered.

"I do not think Haitians are afraid of working hard. They just can't find any job in Haiti. Just go to Croix des Bossales, Iron Market, or any open-air market, you will see how they are pushing or pulling the pushcard loaded with bags and baskets of fruit. Madan Saras would not be able to exist without them," said Viviana.

"I am happy to hear how Madan Saras, street vendors, female entrepreneurs are regarded by the educated class. All of us had a mother, a grandmother or an aunt who was a Sara. Is that what we want for our daughters? We would like something else. Gender-based violence is all too common at the marketplace. Pick-pockets and thieves are abusing Saras. We are not protected by the government," Gigi opened up after a few glasses of rum.

In less than one hour, Christèle's parents sent a grandson to check on her and find out whether she would stop by the house. She knew the time had come for her to thank the Balthazars.

The Journey of Life

The Desperate Trek of Waves of Migrants towards the North

The Queen of the Market Survives the Crossing to Talk about Loss, Death, and Deportation

Mass migration has emerged as a major global story of our time. Human beings from many corners of the world are looking for all kinds of dream. Columbians, Peruvians, Bolivians, and Brazilians have been looking for their own version the Chilean Dream. At one point, Spaniards, Portuguese, Peruvians, Panamanians, Central Americans were looking for their Brazilian Dream. Since the massive earthquake of January 12, 2010 killing thousands of Haitians, Haitians started looking for their Brazilian Dream too. But when the Brazilian economy slowed down, Haitian migrants set sail towards the North.

Christèle started seeing some of her clients leaving Brazil. She knew she had to follow them. She knew there were Haitians who were stuck in many Central American countries. The few migrants who could purchase products to cook could earn money. That's how she started traveling with a group of women and their children. They were following the migrants who came from South and Central Americas, Asia, and Africa.

Crossing Nicaragua and Costa Rica was not easy at all for most of the migrants. Amidst all the hardship encountered in those countries, there were good Samaritans who offered quick shelter, water, clothes, and food to the migrants. The jungle crossing was not something most families with children were ready for. They were traveling, walking in the high mountains, crossing deep and wild rivers. On many occasions, they had to leave comrades behind. Snakes were their most vicious enemies. Christèle stated that pregnant women suffered the most. Once they were bitten by snakes in the middle of the jungle, they were left for dead. In the jungle, there are no doctors, no surgeons, no OB-GYN nurses to help save the unborn. Family members and children had to move on with the rest of the group. On some occasions, children got lost in the jungle. Then, migrants would run into crying children. They were afraid, hungry, malnourished and weak.

"What was the most difficult were the children abandoned in the jungle. If gang members, troops were making a raid, parents ran into hiding. They left their children behind. Other women and young women became the parents of those abandoned kids. They carried them along the way," said Christèle, wiping tears off her eyes.

Christèle took a few minutes to calm down. "We could not stop crossing mountains. Each time, we would find bones of cadavers. There were jumping vipers, lots of coral snakes, fer-de-lance, stinging plants, and biting insects. Some of the travel companions would fall sick of malaria, dengue fever, diarrhea. People were walking without any directions. They were talking to themselves. It was as if they were schizophrenic. Here we were in the wild with sick people!"

The travelers and victims came from many foreign countries. They came from many South Asian countries , other Latin American countries, and many African countries. People perished in the mountains due to continuous exposure, lack of potable water and food. The mountains were too steep. So they rolled down into ravines. Yet, there was fresh water in the jungle. The migrants drank from the rivers at their own risk.

"Far away, you could smell the decomposition of the bodies under the green leaves of the trees. Nobody had time to bury them. On many occasions, they were tired. They wanted to take a nap, but they never woke up. They fell asleep and never woke up. From Turbo, Colombia, the migrants started traveling towards the Darien mountain to arrive in Panama. Many of them will not make it," said Christèle.

On the road, the migrants had to rely on their unscrupulous coyotes and jungle dwellers to cross rivers and lakes. On some occasions, the same guides and police will harass them and force them to give them everything they had. Despite the fact that they had already sold everything they had at home to go on this journey, now they did not have anything left. Some of them had to start using the clothes found on the road. After all, after so many days of traveling and due to fatigue, many travelers threw their own clothes away. Some left them with a note, "I could not carry these clothes with me. If you can use them, please take them. Share with others."

Right in the middle of the river, the coyotes often asked the travelers to get off the boat. If they wanted to continue or cross the river, they needed to pay an additional amount. Despite the exorbitant cost, the migrants pooled in and managed to pay the coyotes for the final leg of the trip. And that would not take them close to their final destination which was the US. – Mexico border.

All across Latin America, the migrants encountered thieves and gang members who controlled the passage. They needed to pay them to cross. Bandits and gang-infested toughs had been fighting for the control of territories. Migrants had to cross gang-infested places in Honduras, El Salvador, and Colombia.

"It was always good to be with a large group," said Christèle. "Especially for the women, it was safer. But it was not always safe everywhere. Over the months, I figured out how to carry the small amount I had. I carried it on my body in very different strategic areas. But other female migrants had to be completely searched. In Nicaragua, I can say some of the authorities are not human beings. They are armed beasts who were ready to reach into women's private areas to find whatever amount they were carrying. In Costa Rica, I saw Cubans, Indians, Bangladeshis, Africans from Congo, Middle Easterners, and many South Asians who were held hostage. They could not cross."

Once the migrants heard gunshots, they started running in all directions. That was how parents hid and ended up losing their children in the forest. As the migrants could not stop, they kept moving forward.

"At Turbo, a Colombian port town, many fellow migrants and I stopped to rest and purchase a few supplies. I bought fruits, bags of rice, beans, and fish. I also bought a cauldron, a pan, and some plastic dishes. The fishermen came early to sell their catch of the day. I bought fresh fish," said Christèle.

The Colombian soldiers who were on patrol on that August 2016 day were checking for human traffickers and drug smugglers. It was a sign of relief to see how nice the residents of Turbo were to most of the migrants. They knew that they were only transiting through their town. Out of that short transit, they were earning some money. Once rested, the migrants would have to start on the next leg of their trip. They would have to start by taking a boat. Then, they would walk to cross the Darien Gap, a 60-mile area of dense jungle between Colombia and Panama.

"Nobody could prepare us for the difficulty of that crossing. There was not a path, a road we were following. We did not know where were going most of the time. We heard crazy animal voices. We had to walk quickly in fear of being caught by the authorities, attacked by jaguars, bandits, and drug growers. We were just crossing their territory. All of a sudden, an Indian migrant fell and rolled into a ravine. His buddies called him, but he did not respond. Either he was knocked out or he died right away. His friends rejoined us. The steep mountains we had to cross caused many to fall behind," said Christèle.

In the middle of the Darien Gap jungle, there was a small clearing that allowed the migrants to rest for a while. Both men and women looked for firewood so they could start some fire to dry their clothes. What they needed the most were water and foods. After so many days in the hellish parts of the crossing, they were hungry and weak.

Christèle and her aides had salt, rice, and beans. They realized that all they needed was to stay in contact with their stomach. With fire, they could boil water from the nearby stream and they could cook the rice. All the men who volunteered to carry the supplies were sure to receive something to eat. Needless to say they had to throw away most of what they had bought in Turbo, Colombia. The steepness of the mountains did not call for them to carry heavy loads. It required them to carry the least amount of supplies. In that clearing, the migrants knew they had to boil more water to carry along the rest of the journey. They knew that if they wanted to make it to the US.- Mexico border and ultimately the United States, they had to rehydrate their body. They did not want to be left behind. They did not want to start suffering from jungle fever and other diseases.

All around the campfire, men and women from many countries were laying exhausted on the ground. Smokes were arising from different areas on the grass-covered space. They were far away from civilization, far away from what was common and familiar. Amidst this group of migrants, there were various subgroups of South Asians such as Indians, Bangladeshis, Nepalese, Pakistanis, Eritreans; West Africans from countries such as Nigeria, Mali, Niger, Gambia, Senegal, Guinea, Ivory Coast, Ghana, and Cameroun; contingents of Central and South Americans; a large subgroup from Congo; and subgroups of Cubans, Haitians, and Jamaicans.

As always, Christèle took the opportunity to chat with the fellow migrants who wanted to tell their stories. It was evident that most of them were able to communicate either in English, Spanish, or Portuguese besides their mother tongues. Depending on how many months they spent in Brazil, Costa Rica, Nicaragua, Peru, Colombia or Bolivia, they may have caught some Spanish or Portuguese. Christèle realized that many of them had enough Spanish and English to make themselves understood. She was able to figure out that those migrants may have been the crème de la crème from their countries. Or it could be that they spent many years working and saving money to take the second leg of their journey. And for many migrants, it could be multiple steps of their journey.

"My wife, son, and I left Nepal three years ago. We flew to Quito, Ecuador. To do so, we had to sell our home and property. We also borrowed some money because our traffickers told us the journey would cost a lot. They charged $3500 to help us get tickets to Ecuador. They said that Ecuador was receiving migrants. Its border was open. That was in 2013. After arriving, we connected with another network of smugglers who guided us to El Salvador. That is where I lost my wife to gang members. She was kidnapped by what I thought were militia groups. So my son and I had to stay there for a while, trying to find a way to buy her freedom," said Mustafa Mohan, wiping tears off his face. His son approached him and laid his right arm on his shoulder.

"We were there for months trying to negotiate with those gangsters. Each time they promised to release her, we paid the amount they requested, but they never released her. We could not ask for help from the authorities. They threatened us and her. We wanted her to come out alive. We did not know where we were in the jungle of El Salvador. The emotional terror we went through was worse. Each night was different. They threatened they would cut her fingers and toes. The threats continued. They threatened they would sell her to other horrible gangs to get the money we could not afford to pay," said Mustafa.

"Could you not find assistance from the trafficker who brought you from Ecuador?" asked Christèle.

"He was long gone. We were alone. We were in a foreign land, but in a jungle with gangsters who live off people on the move. After negotiating with them for 4 months, I told my son that we had to find a way to escape from this hellish place. One night in May 2013, we escaped by walking all night to nowhere. We found ourselves deeper in the mountain amidst howler monkeys, jaguar, hairy tarantula spiders, caiman crocodilus, crocodiles, racer and poisonous snakes of all colors, falcons, flying monkeys crashing on tall tree branches etc. Needless to say we were very afraid. In the mangroves, we ran into a group that was heading to the north. We got a ride to the other side."

Christèle encouraged them to be strong in the midst of all these tribulations and adversity. "A son lost his mother. A husband lost his wife," she sighed. "My husband left me for other women."

A migrant from the Nepalese subgroup, Adityanandana (son of the sun) Adripathi (master of the mountains) decided to speak. His was a story of hero who survived avalanche in the mountain while hiking with rich foreign tourists.

"After the 7.8 magnitude quake destroyed our camp, home, and family members in Nepal, I knew I had to do something. I needed to work to rebuild my community. To do so, I needed to go away, as far away as possible to work. I needed to go to the US, Canada or any European countries," said a well-known Sherpa who survived the quake only to find himself unable to take care of his surviving family members.

"Where were you when the quake hit Nepal," asked Christèle, unable to picture the hard work of those unsung heroes of the mountain.

"A group of the best American, Canadian, Japanese, Korean and European hikers were with me and two of my comrade Sherpas. We were waiting for the weather to clear up a bit when the avalanche came. More than 16 Sherpas and climbers perished. Those of us who survived the destruction of the camp became scared of the Himalaya" replied Adripathi. Friends and other climbers often referred to him as Adri for short.

"So you are used to climb and cross these types of crazy mountains, are you not?" asked Christèle.

"Yes, I am a Sherpa. That's what we are known as in our small community. We guide people to the top of the mountain. Mount

Everest and you can name it in the region. People have dreams. One of their dream is to travel to Mount Everest, the second highest mountains in the world, after Mauna Kea on the island of Hawaii," answered Adri.

"Did you have to go to school to learn to be a Sherpa?"

"Well, most of us Sherpas started out as guides in the tourism industry. Others become porters who help foreign climbers carry their loads. Many of us had to go to the Mountaineering School to get our certificate to be able to work and climbing guides. We are the ones who can establish the difference between life and death in the mountain. We advise and guide climbers to keep them out of dangerous fall, caves, and holes. We are the ones who guide them to the various camps and advise them to take a break," replied Adri.

"What brought you into this dangerous work?"

"Sherpas want to give the best education to their kids. They want to feed and take care of their family members. They work on a day rate. Food may be included, but you can negotiate it with them too. Sherpas go to school to learn various languages such as English, Spanish, Japanese, Chinese, French, German, Russian etc. We make sure we are ready to serve our clients," Adri said.

It was time for the Gambian subgroup to tell their own story. Hassan Kah was the only one who was willing to talk.

"I was born in Mali, but my father was from Niger. So when life started getting more difficult in Mali, the family moved to Niger. That's what my dad wanted. He was a farmer. For many years, he was able to grow enough food for his family and to sell in nearby markets. Our family produced lots of corn, beans, sweet potatoes, yams, and millet. In addition, we had livestock. But when the jihadists started crossing over, we realized we had made a huge mistake. They were running away from Mali."

"Hey, do not forget to tell them about who the Jihadists were," a fellow Malian said, after raising his hand and voice.

"Well, that's right. Boko Haram (against books, i.e. its goal is to overthrow the western education of Nigeria by killing and destroying anything that stood against them. Boko Haram pledged allegiance to ISIS," said Hassan Kah.

"So it is the same terrorist group that kidnapped the Nigerian girls. The news made headlines all over the world," said Adripathi.

"Yes, you are right. Boko Haram terrorized, attacked, and killed the civilian people of northeastern Nigeria. Then, they decided to go to Mali to terrorize Malians. UN, African, and French forces came to fight them. Boko Haram got spread all over Cameroon and other Western Africa," said Hassan.

Christèle decided to take a break to go to the cauldron. She checked the beans and rice. They were all done. She offered a small portion to everybody. She told Hassan to keep telling his story. She offered some cooked rice to the rest of the African migrants.

"Under attack, people become refugees. They wanted to protect themselves against the random attacks inflicted upon them by the Boko Haram terrorists. They even infiltrated the refugees fleeing to nearby shelter. They burned men, women, and children alive. They even shoot our livestock. They kill our goats which are our little banks. They rode around town in small pickup trucks. They carry heavy weapons. I could not take it any longer. My father told me that I had to save myself. By then, I knew that I had to stay away from this constant persecution," said Hassan, a skinny man who appeared to take anything the world had to offer to him.

All of a sudden, another group of men on the move arrived from the jungle. They carried bad news. They were talking about all the bodies they saw in the jungle. They got scared because they did not know who shot them or how they died.

"We were robbed along the way. We were kidnapped by highway thieves and robbed by so-called police officers who stole our money, phones, and eyeglasses," said a few Cuban and Haitian migrants. "We were quiet for a few hours and we were watching you from the jungle. We wanted to make sure that you guys were legitimate migrants like us."

Everybody kept quiet and was surprised by the arrival of this group. They wanted to find out whether they had encountered any authorities who may have been pursuing them. They reaffirmed the new group of migrants that they had left some buddies behind. Some of them got sick and could not continue on the journey. Others broke their legs, got bitten by poisonous snakes. A large group of them was attacked by wild beasts of the Darian Gap.

The men and women of the new group started cooking their meals right away. Christèle let them use some of her supplies because she knew that she could buy new ones in Panama City.

Hassan seized the opportunity to finish telling his story. He wanted to let others know that he did not know any jungle like those they have been crossing. He was a city dweller in his hometown.

"Climate change causes lack of rain. Terrorism brought by Boko Haram and famine caused me to leave. My parents could no longer grow the crops they used to grow. I needed a future. So they sold some of their livestock and gave me the money to travel. The hope was that if I make it to the US, then some day I will be able to help them and the rest of the family. My goal is to go to the US or Canada," said Hassan.

Hassan was part of the migrants who did not want to take the Mediterranean Sea. He took a bus that dropped him off in Agadez, Niger. Then, he paid a trafficker to take him to Algeria. Crossing the long desert while being hungry and thirsty was not easy. He saw many of this traveling companions perishing. Hassan wondered whether it was worth risking his life only for a dream, the American Dream. After arriving in Algeria, he was contacted by some smugglers who told him that Ecuador was the safest way to start his journey to the U.S.- Mexico border. That was the most they could offer to him. All he needed to do was to pay the high fees.

"Here I was in Agadez, a city of people from many countries," said Hassan. "I saw everybody was en route to somewhere. It was like a bunch of ants traveling and carrying their goods. People were looking for their dream in this city of dreams. If the nomads and traders had made it, why not us, migrants from all over the world? I looked around and realized I was surrounded by all kind of people, drivers, sex workers, police officers who were trying to live off us. Agadez exists thanks to people traveling through its station and using its mud-brick compounds with high walls and blazing bright metals. I knew I had to be careful. I could not trust the harem of smugglers who were offering all kind of services. From food, hotel rooms, money exchange, phone chargers and SIM cards for their phones, to prostitutes and nuns dealing marijuana and heroin, the smugglers were able to put migrants in contact with their network setup over many years in many foreign countries."

"All of us here want to try our luck. Nobody can guarantee us that reaching the U.S.- Mexico border will ultimately facilitate our entry into the US or Canada. At least, we will be able to make friends and to know other people from all over the world in this journey," Christèle, as she moved away from the group. She wanted to collect some of her supplies as the first group of migrants wanted to get on the way. There was no time to lose.

The clouds were moving fast in the sky. The migrants wanted to get to their Panama City destination where they could find a decent shelter, recharge their cell phones and call their parents for additional money. Some of the migrants knew friends or had family members living in the USA or Canada. They were watching them along this long and treacherous journey.

"The worst thing is that we were like blinds who were following blinds. We got lost in the tropical jungle and we were crossing the same river over 1,000 times," said Hassan to Christèle. Both of them started laughing with the rest of the traveling party. "We have become a migrating people because there is no stability, no work in the country. I have seen so many migrants aging 16 and 45 years old that the country has just lost a major part of her generation. We become vulnerable travelers who are extorted by gang members all along the route."

"I agree with you. The same can be said about Haiti. The young as well as the old people are leaving the country. Haiti is losing a generation of great brain. What will its future be without young men and women?" said Christèle. "It's a country of broken, shattered dream. Once one leaves his or her country, there are three constant, certain things to find along the way: Misery, Arrival, or death."

"What I have seen during the journey is the humanity and the kindness of fellow travelers. There were many times I also witnessed unity, selfishness, and kindness. People are moving to the Promised Land despite the uncertainty of life in the US. Many migrants prefer that uncertainty to anything in their homeland. To avoid being bullied and ostracized, Africans hope to become blacks in the U.S. Brazilians, Hondurans, and many other South and Central American migrants will fold into the Hispanic or Latino group, or will pass for whites. But Asians will remain Asians. Some of us Indians and Nepalese may be confused for Chinese" said Adripathi as her hurried to catch up with the group.

"Haitians just like you, Nepalese and African brothers, we are people who walk to every destination. We have been able to build mental and physical toughness over the years. We are used to being exposed to the natural elements, but we never had to walk and travel for weeks and months. Some of us started traveling from our home country to Brazil or Ecuador. We crossed Peru, Equador, and Colombia. Here we are in this inferno, this long jungle."

After walking two nights and two days, the traveling migrants arrived in Panama. They found a $3.00 per night no-frill hotel that was already crowded. The owner of the hotel managed to accommodate the group. Some of them reconnected with fellow travelers who were separated from them. They shared news about other travelers who got sick and died along the way. Depending on which country the migrants were from, the name of the hotel could change every week or every month. It went from Mama Cuba to Mama Africa to Mama Honduras or Mama Salvador, Mama America to Mama Haiti. Mama...catered to migrants on their long journey to the U.S.- Mexico border. Mama... provided them with comfort even if it was for a short time. The hotel's owner and staff even said that they were in the business of comforting people who were far away from home and loaded with fear and insecurities. Mama... dealt with contemporary immigration issues. Mama welcomed people who were experiencing a universal human longing. Migrants were longing for this better place, but they were also feeling displaced and longing backwards at the same time. They were outsiders longing to get in, unsure of what they would give up, what they were willing to give up or unwilling to give up. They became the migrating people of hope and promise. Some of them grew up with the promises of the American Dream sold by American movies and shows. They grew up watching TVs. They had been dreaming about getting into the Promised Land. Their eyes had seen it. They had dreamed about it, but they had nothing about living on the streets of this land. As their parents and ancestors had done in the past, they continued to move. Movement always brought blessings. They were the people of movement. Their desperation in their homeland is their preparation for the revelation of a better place to come.

On Sunday mornings, former adherents to Voodoo, Vodoun, Vodou, Shamanism, Santeria, Curanderia as well as catholic faithful gathered to pray in the front yard before leaving Mama America. That time, there were more migrants from the American continent than Africa and Asia combined. They were praying for success on their journey. They were praying so the US could let them go through the San Ysidro Port of Entry. They were praying to get closer and closer to the entry to San Diego. They prayed for those left behind, for those who continued to support them along the journey, for safety and security.

Through texts, Facebook, and WhatsApp, most of those migrants have already found out that Panama and Nicaragua crossings are the most dangerous. Each one of them could tell the stories of friends and family members who were robbed by gang members or police officers who pretended to be coyotes. Some of those bad guys were in cahoots with the real bandits because they saw the source of the money. Needless to say that the migrants who lost their money ended up waiting for more money to arrive from family members to continue the journey. On some occasions, they had to rely on the same thieves to guide them to a place where they could wait.

Walking in the slashing tropical rainfall and under the burning sun in the desert taught the travelers to become one with Mother Nature. Many of them had never set foot in any jungle before this crossing. They had never lived with the natural elements. In the middle of the jungle in the heat of the summer months, all living creatures were wide awake. The birds were chirping during the whole day. Not too far from where they were, the travelers could hear the cascading of the river water. But when nightfall came, they were plunged in deep darkness. This was the time when the mountain dwellers fared better than the city dwellers. The latter were used to living off the land without any running water, electricity, and convenience of the towns. They knew of the importance of shade trees in the jungle. That's why they never hesitated to rest amidst the wide and tall roots of the Ceiba or Mapou trees. The vodou/voodoo adherents found a tall root to change into their white dress and headdresses. In a few minutes, all the women were ready to worship their spirits or loas. They were dancing and singing. The male migrants from many African countries, from Haiti, Brazil, and South and Central Americas joined the night celebration. On the other side of the tree, amidst its tall roots, were the evangelical migrants who were singing hymns. They were also praying for a safe passage to the U.S.-Mexico border. The vodou adherents did not have drums to play but they were clapping their hands and beat the few remaining cooking pans and cauldrons they had. Since they could not bring heavy supplies, once they finished cooking in a resting spot, they left them for the next group of migrants. Under the canopy of the Kapok/Ceiba tree, the migrants felt safe. After celebrating and dancing around the bonfire, they fell asleep early to be able to get back on the road the next day. No matter how much they wanted to celebrate and communicate with their ancestors, they did not want to make too much noise because they feared to attract the attention of the drug cartels whose territory they were crossing. The narco traffickers were running the jungle and surrounding communities.

Considered sacred by past and present cultures and civilizations such as Taïno, Mayan, and Aztec, the Ceiba or Mapou tree has long been associated with the spirit world of the dead. Spirits tend to inhabit those majestic trees. In the middle of the night, the native Indians joined the migrants' celebration. Even the migrants from Asia joined them too.

The celebrants and migrants left their candles and other items in the crevices and on the buttresses of the Mapou tree, also known as silk cotton tree. On those hot summer nights, they did not have to worry about wild animals that would come to attack them in the middle of the night. The large crevices and buttresses of the ceiba tree gave them protection on the floor of the jungle. Its large canopy also gave them protection from the heat of the day. However, their celebration did not last long.

Bad people smugglers, coyotes for the Spanish speaker or passeurs for the French speakers sometimes got lost on purpose just so the migrants could become more dependent on them. They had a hard time guiding the tech-savvy ones who depended on their cellphone or were using Google to find the right route. They got upset and warned the region's gang members, drug cartels, and native dwellers of the upcoming passing of those tough city dwellers scattered in the jungle.

"Gunmen descended on a group of migrants. We happened to find some of them running away from the migrants," said Hassan. "So we changed route. We could not bear seeing women being strip-searched by those gunmen who became more aggressive. Once they saw an item in the woman's private area, maybe a pad, they beat up the woman because they thought she was hiding money. The gunmen took the pad at gunpoint and pushed it towards their associates who saw the blood. The female migrant had her menstruation."

The Managua, Nicaragua gunmen took advantage of their country's closure of their borders. Over the months and years, migrants have learned to avoid this route. At the same time, many of those migrants will inform others of the countries that facilitated their passage. Costa Rica and Honduras were two of them that gave them permits to cross. That's why many Cubans, Asians, Africans, and Haitians ended up spending weeks in Costa Rica. Migrants who were caught in Nicaragua were returned to Costa Rica or were forced to pay $1,000 to let them go through the country.

"Yes, we all can say we crossed hell. Hell is on earth. The Darien Gap was hell for most of us. But when we crossed the Suchiate River on those floating planks, we knew we were close. We crossed from the Guatemala side of the river to the Mexico side. The coyote guide dug his long stick into the river as the waves pushed by the wind almost wrecked the inner tube," said Christèle, looking at the Mexican side of the river.

Passengers rolled up their pants and dresses and jumped over to disembark the tubes. They climbed up in the muddy area until they reached the other side of the river. Those who could take a taxi or a motorcycle ride paid their fares. They wanted to get to Tijuana, Mexicali or the Mexican office which could issue them a 20-day pass. Most importantly, they wanted to be as close to the San Ysidro Port of Entry. They wanted to enter the US through San Diego. Then, they would go to wherever their friends and family members lived. Wanting something is always different from getting it. The migrants' journey was always full of risks, losses, and death. It was always a huge gamble. And many of them will never make it to the Promised Land. But it was not because of lack of trial and tribulations. They gave it all they got. They gave it time, money, luck, sweat, blood, lost limbs, loss of relationship, marriage, loss of family members and children. They were even ready to face loss of all their resources and death.

The Traveling Sisters of the Higher Purpose Shelter

Months later, Rose and Carline were found at the Higher Purpose Shelter run by non-Catholic nuns who were focused on growing weeds to heal and provide comfort to the migrants. The Traveling Sisters of the Higher Purpose Shelter were not real nuns. But nobody cared about whether or not they were fake nuns. They were doing something good for the needy and the poor traveling migrants. They were feeding and healing the thousands of migrants who came to their door in Tijuana and Mexicali, Mexico. The Traveling Sisters were always wearing their clergy robe any time they were outside working in their marijuana fields. They wanted to produce enough cannabis so they could heal all kinds of physical ailments with their concoctions. Making cannabis lotions and oils allowed them to reach out to the sick and poor migrants.

Cannabis lotions and oils are what kept the two sisters busy. Sister Petra and Sister Tetra grew up from their huge family farms. They had brothers who would work with their parents in the field. They were never encouraged to work alongside their parents. But Sister Petra and Sister Tetra had another calling. They wanted to teach their parents a lesson. They absorbed all the growing techniques from observing their parents' grow seasons. They agreed to call their business ' PetraTetra Spiritual Oils and Lotions' or PETRASOL. PETRASOL products were made with marijuana strains that offer a high concentration of

CBD, one of the primary cannabidoids found in marijuana. Sister Petra and Sister Tetra recognized that CBD does not have any huge psychoactive effects. However, they were able to recognize that it has a lot of great medicinal benefits. Both sisters had seen enough people complaining of all sorts of pain. They figured out that their lotions and oils could not only diminish their pain but also help them feed the hungry, homeless, and sick.

Sister Petra could not say no to people. She could not turn their back on these two girls who arrived at her Higher Purpose shelter. Even though the shelter was overcrowded, she managed to find a bed for them. Two female migrants brought them to the shelter. That's all they could do for these two girls, Carline and Rose.

Sister Petra never stopped asking them about their parents. She was heart-broken when the girls started telling them their stories.

"Our parents abandoned us near a bonfire in the swampy, insect-infested jungle of Panama. We were waiting for the next boat ride when some gang members or narco traffickers or the authorities conducted a raid of our area," said Carline who has grown up amidst the tribulations of the long journey from Brazil.

"All of a sudden, we heard gunshots in the middle of the Darien Gap. Our parents started running away in one area. They told us to run away in the other direction. Carline and I tried to stay together," said Rose.

"Did you run away by yourselves? Were you following other migrants?" Sister Petra asked, shocked.

"Rose and I were following some other migrants. We ran, fell, got up, got stuck in the swamp. We did not want to get shot. The narco growers and drug traffickers wanted to kill us. Maybe we were crossing their territory. That's what some people said," Carline said.

"Did your parents try to find you? Did they look for you?" asked Sister Tetra.

"It would be very difficult to find us. We were running in one direction. They were running in the opposite direction. I do not know whether they got shot in the back. I saw other dead bodies along the way," replied Carline.

Sister Petra and Sister Tetra reached out and hugged the girls. "You do not have to worry. We will take care of you. God brought you to us. And here at the Traveling Sisters of the Higher Purpose Shelter, we never turned away people in need," said Sister Tetra.

"You will be part of our growing family. We will take care of you. We will feed you, clothe you, and provide you with shelter. And if your parents survived the crossing, some day, you will see them again," Sister Petra said to the girls as she held their hands

"Do not worry. Tonight after dinner, we will have a bonfire. I will invite some friends and all the other migrants who are staying here. I will ask you to tell your stories. Will you be able to tell your stories?" asked Sister Tetra.

"Yes. We will." Both girls nodded their head. They looked at each other and deep down realized they were rescued. But they did not know whether this rescue would ever reunite them with their parents. They did not know whether the parents survived and stayed at a shelter in Rosarito or Mexicali or Tijuana.

"Can you promise us to help us look for our parents?" asked both girls. Carline and Rose figured out that they had a good chance of finding their parents some day. Telling their stories of their desperate trek will put them in the news. News media will rebroadcast their stories.

The sisters realized that while migrants are waiting to cross over the border between Mexico and the US, they would need to earn money. Many of them had a long history of working in the field in their homeland. Many of them came from countries where they used to grow marijuana and cocaine.

Wearing their white robes with golden bibs, the two sisters, Sister Petra and Sister Tetra, were recruiting men and women who could work, cook, and clean. They needed to make good use of their plot of land. They wanted to make their parents proud of their ranch production. Sister Petra and Sister Tetra did not want to compete against the established drug cartels in that part of Mexico. They only wanted to do God's work by growing enough Cannabis plants to be able to produce their PETRASOL merchandise. And to build a better source of income, the Sisters followed specific guidelines. They knew they could sell their oil and lotions in the US and the rest of the world as Hemp products. Thanks to a 2004 case the Hemp Industry Association won against the DEA, the Sisters wanted to follow the formulas showing small traces of THC, the chief psychoactive cannabidoid. Growing up in California and attending graduate school in Colorado, the two Sisters knew exactly that to ship their legal products within the US or to US consumers, they had to contain no more than 0.3 percent concentration of THC. In addition, while living in Colorado, both sisters were able to obtain their Medical Marijuana cards, allowing them to grow legally.

Over the past few years, the Traveling Sisters of the Higher Purpose Shelter were able to help migrants with chronic back pain, broken limbs, grand mal seizures, migraine, anxiety, depression, insomnia, acne, personality disorder, inflammation, headaches and many other ailments. In their Inbox, they kept the feedback and comments they received from customers living in South and Central Americas, the Caribbean, the US, Africa, and Europe. Many customers wrote that their oil and cannabis salve performed miracles on their bodies. Keep in mind that the Traveling Sisters did not promote their oil and lotions this way. Customers wrote back to them to inform them of the healing power of their oil and lotions. Melted with the oil, the beeswax acts as a preservative.

Despite their best efforts to remain simple, the two Sisters were often told that they were in the wrong business. No matter what they were told by the naysayers, the two nuns continued to do God's work. But when they were approached by some drug dealers and cartel members, they knew what to tell them. Even their own parents and family members criticized them for being fake nuns going into this type of business. To each group, the two Sisters said that their cannabis were like the anointment Jesus used during his earthly ministry. They kept pushing forward. Despite all the setbacks they had encountered, they were encouraged by the visits of a few Catholic priests who told them they had always wanted to do what they were doing.

Sister Petra and Sister Tetra continued to feel motivated by the huge number of migrants they received at the Traveling Sisters of the Higher Purpose Shelter. The stories they told them around the nightly bonfire made them feel that it was worth working hard to help their fellow men and women. They knew they could not do it all by themselves. They needed some manpower. They ended up hiring a ranch manager, foreman, and drivers.

It was the end of the Sisters' work day. They worked hard in their garden. It was the time for them to clean their hands and change their robes dirtied not only by the mud and dust but also by all the migrating children who enjoyed hugging them.

"We want more stories. Are we going to have a bonfire," asked the kids playing in the front yard of the shelter.

"Yes, for sure. Invite your friends. We will have tea and coffee," said Sister Petra.

"Tell your parents to bring you. Do not come alone. You will not be able to walk back by yourselves. You can tell us your own stories," said Sister Tetra.

Chapter 6

Three hours later, more migrants continued to arrive. The Traveling Sisters of the Higher Purpose Shelter became overwhelmed. It became difficult to have 10 people sleep in one bedroom. Sister Petra and Sister Tetra had to start turning people around. They gave them the names of the nearby shelters to go to. As the migrants were not given appointments to plead their cases with the US officials, they ended up staying longer at the Traveling Sisters' HP Shelter.

"It has been very difficult for us to say no to needy people. We had to make a decision. All of their stories were almost the same. The economy tanked. As Brazil's economy continues to spiral further into the depths of its worst crisis in generations, more workers are leaving. Mexican shelters have been inundated ever since," said Sister Tetra.

"That's why they have started to start their oil and lotion business to be able to feed and shelter the migrants," said Sister Petra.

When Sister Petra and Sister Tetra were approached with a business idea, they quickly acted on it. With their own savings, they invested into a nice property which needed to TLC worker to turn it into an upper scale restaurant. They had to develop a business plan that would attract not only local paying consumers but also migrants. Their business plan was also accepted by a few angel investors who contributed into the launch of this one-of-a-kind restaurant. The way to earn money to help the growing local homeless and traveling migrants was to charge paying customers at breakfast and lunch to be able to reopen at night to serve the homeless and migrants.

Sister Petra and Sister Tetra named their new business venture 'Sisters Restaurant.' They thought they would not have clients and chefs to cook for them. They have been surprised by the number of rich people who make reservations months and weeks early to be able to have breakfast and lunch at Sisters Restaurant. This way, they were able to feed the homeless and migrants in the evening. Ever since Sisters

Restaurant opened its door to the public, it has been busy. Reservations were booked for months. Charge the rich or those who were able to afford it to feed the growing homeless population and traveling migrants.

"Charge the rich to feed the poor has become our mission. And there are a lot of professional business people, industrialists, government workers, diplomats, and even international celebrities who have made reservations to eat at our humble restaurant," Sister Petra. They embrace the mission of being messengers of peace and compassion in this hectic world. Most of these people who come from all the corners of the world may never have to enter the United States, but we have a way of welcoming and making them feel accepted in our country."

"Yes, being granted an appointment to plead their case with the US officials does mean they will be able to stay in the US. Many of them will be loaded onto a plane to be deported to their country of origin. What's interesting is that many of them had to sell everything they had to try to get to the border between the US and Mexico. They will have to decide whether it is worth returning home poorer or staying here to try to make a living in Mexico," said Sister Tetra.

"God had sent the world to our door step. God had sent his own missionaries to Mexico. The homeless and migrants are not all uneducated people. They are educated people who fell on hard economic times. Among them, you will find doctors, teachers, business professionals, merchants, street vendors, Madan Saras or hustlers, people who are trying to do anything to make a living," said a visiting priest to the Sisters Restaurant. The priest was interested in finding out how the Catholic Church of Mexico could help the Sisters Restaurant. As much as he is concerned, charge the rich to feed the homeless and migrants is part of the Mother Church's ministry.

With the funds raised from the angel investors and contributions from the Catholic Church of Mexico, the Sisters Restaurant became the most sought-after breakfast and lunch reservation in Tijuana, Mexico. Sister Petra and Sister Tetra have already started working on an expansion of the building. Several business people and entrepreneurs have already contacted the two Sisters on a franchise.

"We have to reach the border towns first. That's the goal of our mission. That's where God wants us to work with the homeless and migrants. We have plans to expand in Nogales, Mexicali etc," said Sister Tetra.

Paying customers at Sisters Restaurant foot the bill for the migrants and homeless who can dine in the evening. They are attracted by the great meals prepared and served by celebrity chefs who decided to leave their luxury hotel jobs once or twice a week to volunteer there.

Sister Petra and Sister Tetra met with their chefs every morning to discuss the meals. The chefs took their volunteer work seriously. The two nuns thanked them for their dedication to the ministry. They also revealed that they received more requests from other chefs coming from other countries.

"We are happy to share this news with you. Chefs from Brazil, Haiti, Costa Rica, Panama, and even Africa want to work with us," said Sister Petra.

"Our paying customers do not mind trying foods from other countries either. I have noticed that there has been a large request for Brazilian, Cuban, Haitian, and Congolese food. Those who ate Brazilian specialties such as Acarajé, Moqueca Bahiana, Vatapá, Cocadas always made reservations for more. More and more of our paying clients want Haitian French/Spanish/Native/African-based culinary style. They never stopped asking for more Haitian specialties such as Poulet aux Noix (chicken and cashew nuts), Mayi Moulen ak Sòs pwa, poul an sòs (cornmeal with beans and stewed chicken), griyo (fried pork), lanbi an sòs, lanbi Kreyòl (conch in creole sauce), lanbi boukannen, woma boukannen (grilled conch, grilled lobster), Tassot /Taso ak bannann peze (dried fried meat with squeezed fried plantains), Mayi Moulen kole ak legim (cornmeal, beans and vegetables stew), Salad Kreson (Watercress salad), rice with black mushrooms (Diri ak Djon Djon), Rice and beans (Diri Kole or Diri ak Sòs pwa)."

"You forgot to mention Cuban foods. For the past few months, we have been receiving a lot of Cubans who were stuck in Costa Rica and Nicaragua. Our paying customers enjoy eating their arroz con pollo (rice with chicken), carne con papas (meat and potatoes), and the famous Cuban sandwich and La Frita (Cuban hamburger)," said Sister Tetra.

The whole staff members of the Sisters Restaurant were getting for the lunch crowd. In less than 2 hours, those who had made reservations months ahead would be arriving. Sister Petra and Sister Tetra reviewed the list of necessary food items and orders. Without any problem, they reminded their staff to continue to serve their paying clients with dignity. Once again, they did not have to be reminded to provide great customer service. Most of the waitresses had their own stories to tell. They felt privileged to be able to work at The Sisters Restaurant. Most of them were rescued by the Good Shepherd Shelter in Tapachula, Mexico. Back home, they had a great life, but gang warfare chased them. Violent shootings caused them to leave with the clothes on the clothes on their back. They could not show their the terrorist gang members that they were leaving. Most of them had livestock, homes, and other belongings they could not take.

Baja California, especially Tijuana, for many years now, has become the cornerstone of the world. It has become a major international crossing. Way before the border crossings into San Diego started tightening, migrants from South and Central America, Africa, Asia or Southeast Asia and Europe had made Tijuana their favorite destination. From Ecuador and Brazil, they had continue to arrive in the Mexican towns bordering the United States. From 2013, 2014, 2015 and up to 2016, the world was moving. So the two nuns knew exactly what they were dealing with. Comforting and reaching out to the migrants have become part of their mission.

Before the whole lunch crowd started arriving, Sister Petra and Sister Tetra walked around the restaurant to check the tablecloths and cutlery. They do the same run around in the evening before the homeless crowd sit down to eat. "Why not treat the rich and the poor the same even it's just once?" said Sister Petra.

"That's what I like it here. Everybody is treated the same. The two nuns treat the paying clients and the homeless the same way. I heard they are not real nuns. But as far as I am concerned, true nuns have not done a better job than these two here," said Ramona, the cleanliness chief at the restaurant.

"That's why I do not mind being here to cook in the kitchen on my day off from my upscale luxurious hotel job," said Diego who used to work as a well-known chef in Rio de Janeiro before he was fired when the Brazilian economy spiraled into a deep bottom.

"I want my clients to eat with the same dignity as any other client," added Sister Tetra, who stopped her conversation to greet one of her regular customers.

"Life is too short to think it's all about amassing the wealth of this world. How about alleviating the misery of the unfortunate ones, the poor, the migrants in a foreign country?" said Diego. "Brazil did not know how to manage its economy when it was good. Now people are suffering. I was trying to make it to the US, but with the tightening of the border before the end of this administration, I doubt whether I will be able to make it."

"God has a plan for you, Diego. Who says that he did not bring you here to be able to find a better job at the hotel? God works in mysterious ways," said Ramona, a poor woman of no means running away from her own community controlled by gang members.

Way before noon on that beautiful Baja California day, the restaurant was already filled by all of its customers. Rich people who came in to participate in this amazing business model, pay enough to feed the poor while eating their foreign specialties. The atmosphere was very cordial. They were hungry and could not wait for their orders placed months ahead. And the chefs were going to satisfy them to the fullest.

With great fanfare, the waitresses, accompanied by the chefs brought their first course which was an appetizer. The waiting clients salivated and clapped.

"Today, as your first appetizer, you are going to have pwason boukannen (grilled fish), bannann peze (fried plantains), pikliz to water it down (pickled cabbages and vegetables such as onions, carrots, peppers, vinegar etc). All is prepared by our Haitian chef and colleague," said the waitress as the chef bowed, lifted up his head and raised his hand to the clapping of all the clients.

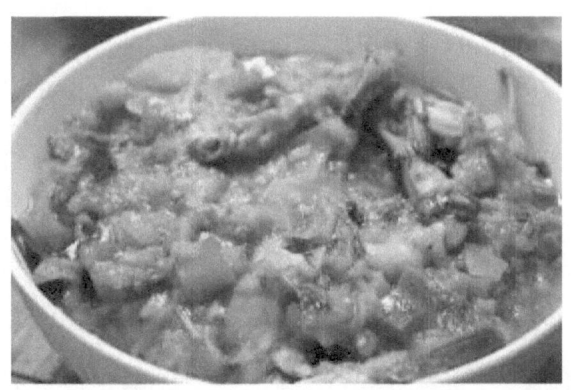

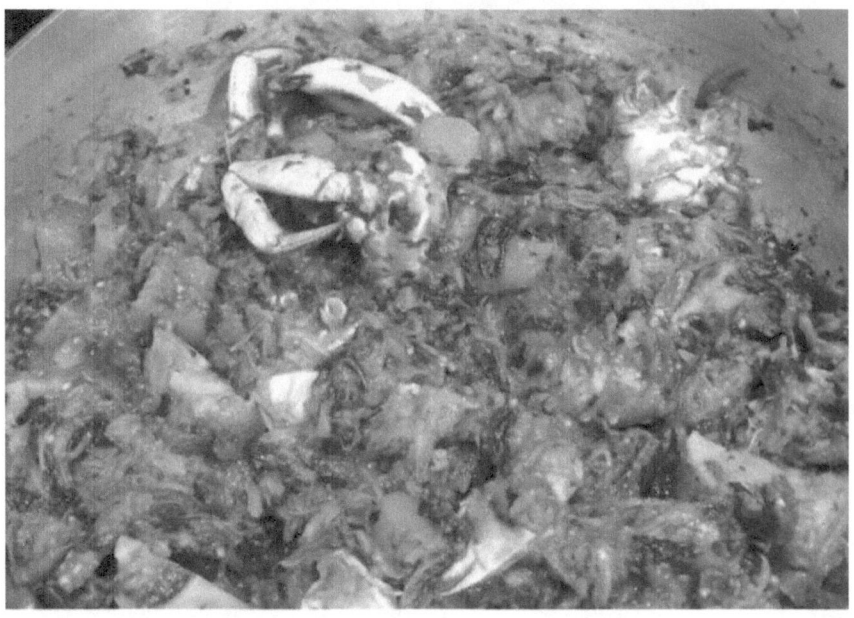

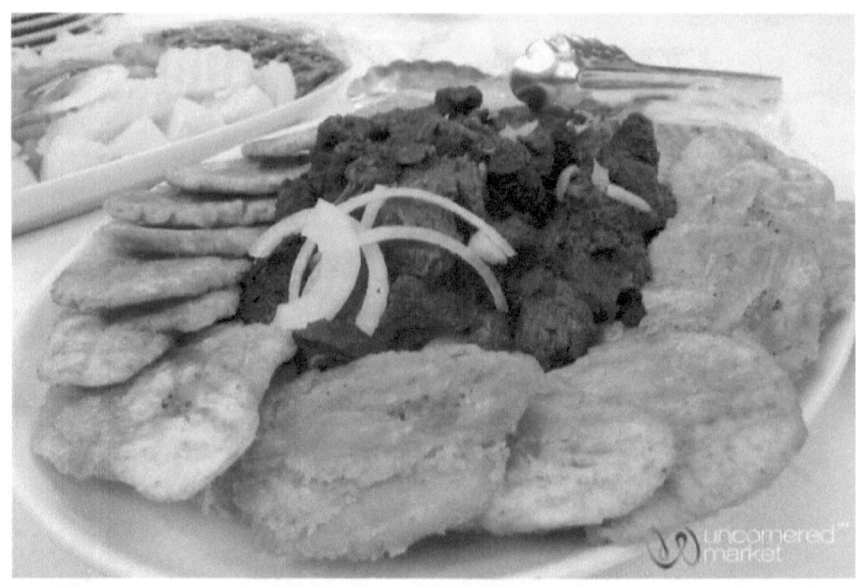

In less than 20 minutes, the other waitress brought a well-decorated tray of fried plantains, *bannann peze,* fried pork, *griyo,* topped off with slices of onion. She introduced the two chefs who prepared this entrée. One was from Salvador de Bahia, Brazil, and the other one was from Havana, Cuba. The Cuban chef, Pablo, was all too happy to answer the questions asked by his guests.

"How long did it take you to prepare this amazing plate?" asked a guest at the table near him

"Since I had already known what I was going to make, I started cooking less than 1 hour ago. My plantains were already peeled and soaked in a light salty solution," replied Pablo.

"How come the fried plantains kept this golden color?" asked a gentleman sitting at the table on his left side.

"Well, cooking requires lots of attention. I let them cook for less than 8 minutes. I turned them in the hot olive oil," answered Pablo.

Cristiano was waiting for his turn. He was the one who was laughing the most. He saw how people were not too familiar with the vegetables of his homeland.

"Can you find plantains all over Cuba?" asked a young girl who was prodded by her father to ask her own question.

"Yes, for sure. Cuba used to be a huge producer of all kinds of plantains. Before the Revolution, Cuba used to export tons of plantains to the US, Canada, and many European countries. Once the embargo was set, the production dropped under the Castro regime. But that does not mean that Cuba does not grow and harvest plantains. It's mostly for the local market,' replied Cristiano.

"How do you know all of those things since you are from Brazil?"

"My mother is from Cuba. My father is from Salvador de Bahia, Brazil. I traveled with my mother to Cuba to visit my grandparents. Cuba maintained a great relationship with Brazil during all those years of the Castro regime. As a young boy growing up, I wanted to be like Fidel Castro. Brazil, especially, my region, produces lots of banana and plantains. The food is top notch in Bahia," replied Cristiano.

"What happened to Brazil before and after the Olympic game?"

"Well, I guess you want to talk about the downfall of the economy. Mismanagement and corruptions destroyed the economy when it was flourishing. Countries will proper if they can trade with their neighbors. That's what ended up landing me here in Tijuana en route to the North. What was I supposed to do after losing my job? I became a migrant just like many of these people," replied Cristiano.

"But the Cubans could enter the US if they wanted to do so during all those years. How come Pablo did not come to Florida?"

"Well, I did not think the 50-plus-year policy allowing Cubans to touch US soil to be granted permission to stay and become citizens of the US would disappear. I guess I took too long. The Castro regime and its boogeymen did not make it easy for people like us with few means to get up and leave. Otherwise, I would have left the island long time ago. I had a government job. I was young. Life was not that bad then," replied Pablo.

"Oh I feel sorry for you to have to deal with all these crossings to enter the US now," said a retired Canadian businessman who had been living in Mexico for more than 10 years.

"Well, thanks. I did not know that Nicaragua would have made our life a living hell in that country. We, Cubans, who did not wait to be asked twice to send our best professional workers, doctors, teachers, engineers to all those countries after they were ravaged by hurricanes, did not think they would mistreat us. Nicaragua ended up closing its border with Costa-Rica right under our nose. We had to live like animals on the border. Thanks to Costa-Rica's government that negotiated with its neighbor, we were able to cross, after paying large sums for the passage. Here we are here stuck again. And things are getting tighter. The Obama administration is planning on terminating the 'Dry foot, wet foot' policy now," said Pablo.

"Now that the US has a new president, will you have a chance to reach your family members in Florida?"

"I doubt I will. The new Republican President of the US wants to keep migrants and refugees out of his country. He wants to build a wall on the border of Mexico with the US. And he wants to make the Mexican president pay for it," said Pablo.

All the guests who heard such a statement started shaking their heads. Others laughed in disbelief.

"You are right. That was one of the main points or promises of his campaign. His position on immigration got him elected," said Panamanian author, Agosto de San Marcos, who had been living in Mexico before the arrest of former Panamanian dictator, Manuel Antonio Noriega Moreno.

"I will blame the ending of 'Pies Secos, Pies Mojados' policy on fellow Cubans who abused it. If you are running from a government, you will not return there after 1 year or 2 years after getting your green cards or citizenship paper. Those fellow Cubans who claimed they were persecuted by the Castro regime destroyed a good thing for the rest of us," said Pablo with indignity. "Now, this is where I landed. I am not saying I will never make a living in Mexico, but it will be harder."

"Have you been trying to cross since you have arrived here?" asked a guest sitting next to him.

"I have been waiting for an appointment with the US officials. I have not been called to plead my case. I do not know which stories to tell them because those officials have already heard them all. Then, less than 5 months later, those who were granted green cards and citizenship, return to Cuba."

Pablo appeared very broken after this long trek from Ecuador, Peru, Columbia, Nicaragua, Costa-Rica, Guatemala and Mexico. He appeared to resign with the American Dream. He was one of the few lucky ones who were able to find a job in their profession. He was able to pay rent in Tijuana until he found his current job. He has thousands of his fellow Cubans who continued to wait for a miracle to happen for them. The Cuban miracle of touching US soil might have lasted more than fifty years. Pablo and his fellow citizens were stuck in all the border towns of Mexico. They were waiting for a Hail Mary touchdown on US soil. They were waiting with all the Central American, Southeast Asians, Africans, Indians, and Haitians.

"Don't give up. Some miracle may happen before January 20, 2017. Keep your chin up. I have seen churches, community centers, after-school programs, private homes, and corridors transformed into shelters to meet the needs of this stream of migrants. This is the time I can say I am proud to be Mexican. The federal employees must be working hard to assist the different committees that erected to feed, shelter, and organize those people in transit," said a couple who never ceased to return for breakfast and lunch. They had long realized that working the Sisters in this business was a good way to face this humanitarian disaster.

The last 2 plates that came to a nearby table were legumes with crabs. The waitress presented it with the rhythm of a popular Konpa song.

"Ladies and gentlemen, you are about to eat one of the best Haitian specialties, Legumes with crabs. Most of our Mexican compatriots have been falling in love with the Haitian cuisine. It's a combination of native Taïno, French, Spanish, and all the cultures that formed Haiti," said the beautiful Mexican waitress, dressed for the occasion. Rich people liked to eat their meals before they touched their palate. From the kitchen where the multinational chefs were doing their magic, the aroma of the Legumes with Crabs attacked the guests.

"Oh la la, this one is my favorite plate," said Cristiano who met a lot of Haitians during his Minustah or UN placement in Haiti right after former Priest who became president, Jean Bertrand Aristide, was sent into exile in West Africa.

"That's the food we ate when we went to Haiti on our honeymoon and later missionary work," said a couple sitting on the corner of the Sisters Restaurant. "We were never able to replicate it when we returned to Mexico. It looks like God sent the best of Haiti to us here."

"Yes. We have some of the best magicians in the kitchen. They are amazing chefs," said the waitress as she placed the large platter in the middle of the table in a rolling center.

Just like any other time, Sister Petra and Sister Tetra walked around to converse with her amazing clients whose belly was full by then. It was an atmosphere of complete joy and hope in this corner of Tijuana. But the minute they stepped outside, they were going to see the sea of humanity that is displayed on the street canvas, sometime right out of the Sisters Restaurant. But those rich people continued to make reservations for next time. That was their way of comforting the poor and the migrants. Through a third party, they were touching the needy the rest of the world seemed to forget about. It was not that the world did not know about the misery and violence in parts of the world. It was because they kept saying those things were happening far from us. They were happening in Iraq, Yemen, Syria and else. When children and babies started washing up on European beaches, the rest of the world started being shocked. When natural disasters such as the 2010 quake devastated Haiti and recent 2016 Hurricane Matthew destroyed Haiti's southern peninsula, the rest of the world started realizing we were all living in the same world and that climate change really existed.

"How did you like your meals today?" asked Sister Tetra at the table near the kitchen.

"Great. I never knew that such great foods existed in those countries. I never paid attention to the culture. I always thought about the misery, the natural disasters, the political upheavals when I see the horrible news about these places. Now that circumstances bring them to us, we start realizing they are just like us," said a gentleman.

"I am very happy to know that you are part of the team who made this possible. We can say it is a reality. This business plan is working. Charge those who can pay for their meals so we can feed the migrants and the local homeless in the evening. And we do both with great style, respect, and dignity," said Sister Petra.

"I am wondering why this is not replicated in other parts of the world or our countries. The few of us who have most of the world's resources should start reaching out to the poor. Now I understand the Robin Hood effect, Sister," said a lady, clutching her wallet while sitting close to her husband.

"Please feel free to take your time to talk. Please return at your next reservation date. The meals will be even better. Who knows who will still be around? We may have new chefs. We have a long list of chefs who are willing to give a few hours of their times to cook in our kitchen. Are we not lucky?" said Sister Petra, shaking her head and erasing sweats from her face.

Baja California was hot and crowded. It seemed to never sleep. It was like any major international cities. "If people can no longer go to New York, then Tijuana and Mexicali or any border towns may replace it," yelled a kid amidst her parents. "The new President will sign Executive Orders to prevent some people from entering the United States. I read it on my Ipad. He will sign Executive Orders to deport undocumented migrants. This is not a good time to go to the US. I have read this on my IPad"

"Do not worry about it," said firmly his mother to the young kid. "We will still be able to visit our family members in Santa Barbara. You are a citizen of the US too."

"How about all these people? The new President does not like people of color. I read it in the news during his campaign. He is not like President Obama who liked everybody, all the good people."

"I said you do not have to worry about it," firmly said his father, hugging him to reaffirm him.

As the clients were leaving the Sisters Restaurant, Ramona dropped by to see what she would have to do to keep it clean. Right before 4 PM, the homeless would start forming lines outside.

"Later tonight, we will have a bonfire. If you have time, you can bring your family to listen to some of the stories our migrants will tell us," invited the two nuns.

"We will try to make it. We would like to hear their stories. We hope to have some new business ideas to share with some of them. If they are going to wait here, they'd better find something to do," said a couple. Fabienne wanted to convince the two nuns to start thinking about job creation to help the migrants stranded in their midst. It was clear to most border dwellers that the waves would end up washing in their interior. They were also wondering whether the Mexican Federal authorities would help the local residents of the border with the costs of sheltering this wave of migrants. Fabienne and her husband knew some key government officials through their various small businesses. They promised they would try to pull strings whenever they could.

"Hey do not forget about the Piñata-making business I shared with you last time, Sister Petra," Fabienne said.

"We have to find jobs for all those young men and women. There are a lot of parents with children here. They need to find a way to take care of themselves. If not, we may have to witness more and more crimes in Tijuana," agreed Sister Tetra.

"You are right, Fabienne. The last thing we do not want to see is a new wave of crimes organized by desperate people who want to survive," said Sister Petra. "We have to use this huge human potential. We should not let go to waste."

"It is far too easy to recruit young men and women who have been sitting around with nothing to do. The Narco lords are sniffing around here. They see lots of desperate migrants who want to get to the so-called paradise. They will offer them jobs as growers, mules, and you name it," said Fabienne whose brother was kidnapped in the heydays of Narco wars and later on executed by a competing drug lord. "I lost my own family members in the drug wars of 1970s and 1980s."

"Migrants and homeless people need shelter, food, clothes, and a decent way of making a living," said Sister Tetra.

"People like my husband and you can make a difference in the midst of this crisis. God brought great human capital and potential to our doorsteps. It is up to us to innovate to absorb this human capital for the development of our border towns. While young men and children go to school, parents can be employed in our local industries. We have to form a grassroots movement to inform our business communities, restaurant owners, farmers, growers, shop owners etc," said Fabienne.

"I concur," said Sister Petra. "The worst thing that can happen to Baja California is not to integrate these people into our society. They are entrepreneurs, merchants, and educated people who only need a helping hand. We only hope that our Federal government will give us some funds to create and support businesses that are sheltering and feeding them. They must open the government-run emergency center if this wave continues. Intergovernmental groups cannot carry these challenges alone. That is why our local citizens are helping."

Chapter 7

The Parliament of the Common Men and Women around a Bonfire

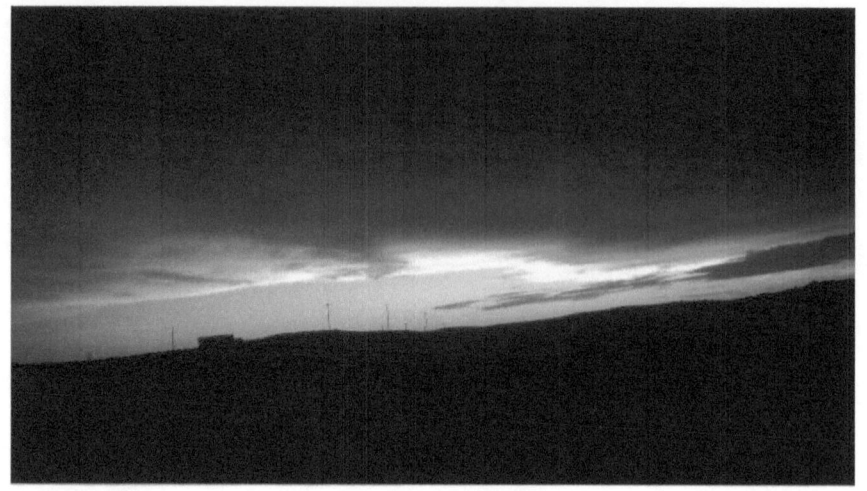

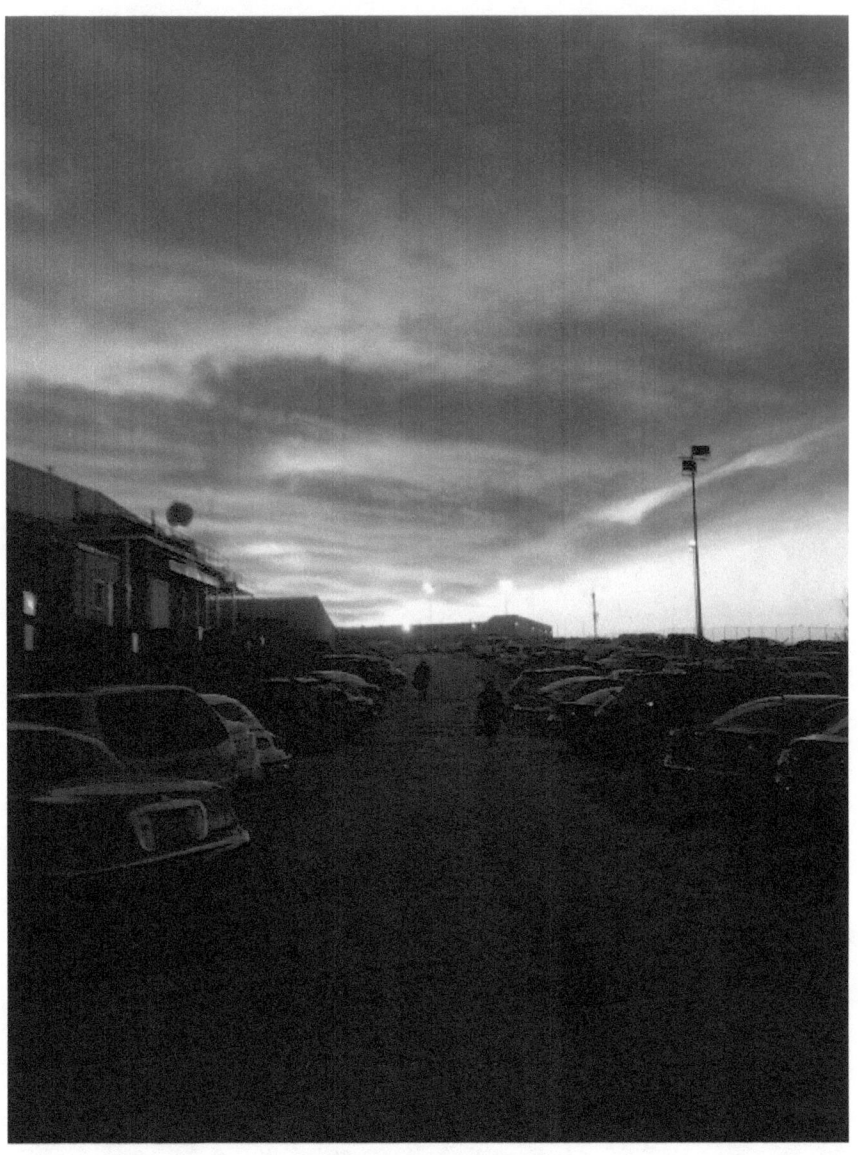

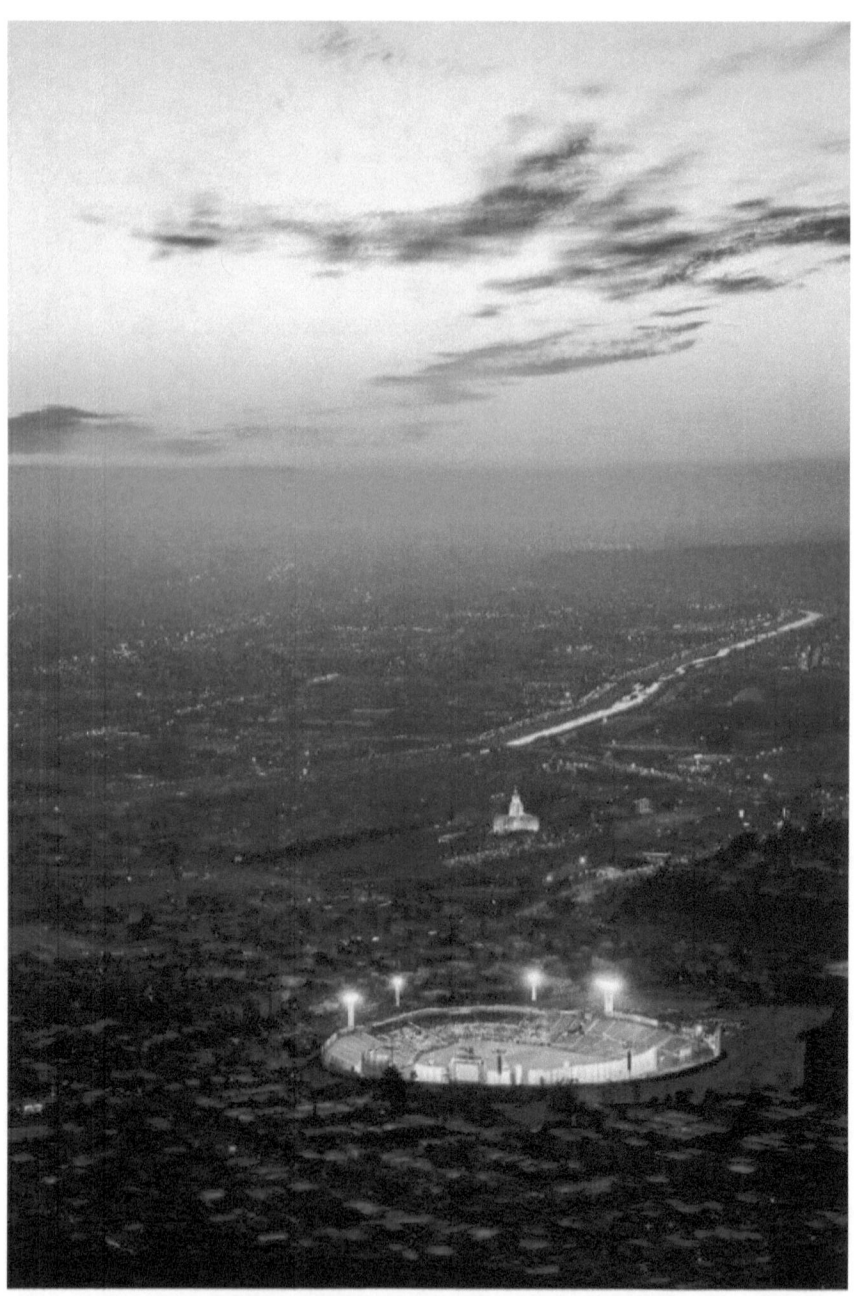

It was a moonlit night in Baja California. Just like any other nights, the residents of Tijuana refused to go to bed. How could they go to bed in a city that never sleeps? Migrants as well as local Tijuanenses were enjoying the great nightlife of this cosmopolitan town. Tourists came from the nearby towns such as Rosarito, Mexicali, Calexico, Bajamar, and even Ensenada. But located at about 11 miles from Tijuana, Rosarito continues to attract the most tourists in Baja California. These tourists needed great food, superb weather, and gorgeous women in a safe environment. Thanks to all its super-chic and low cost hotels, Tijuana had long become the best destination to have fun in the sand and under the Mexican sun. American retirees, Canadian and European travelers have long found a refuge in these coastal border towns. Armed with their $US dollars and Euro, these tourists found Baja California to be an affordable place to live and have fun. After all, they have access to the rest of the world in one spot. Tourists enjoy spending time at Rosarito beach. In the evening, they just drive to the various bars, clubs, discos, and night clubs on Avenida Revolución. That's where most of the college students drive to drink. Mexico's legal drinking age is 18 after all. So LA and San Diego students and business people drive to Tijuana to drink. On any given nights, the hotels, bars, discos, and night clubs that dot the Avenida Revolución are filled with tourists of all ages. Just like any major cities, Tijuana attracts the rich as well as the poor, the migrants from the rest of the world as well as the homeless.

On that moonlit night, the local police were chasing a car thief. He stole an Escalade truck in front of hotel in Rosarita. The pursuit started in the middle of the busy downtown, went around the beachfront before heading to Tijuana. It was a long 10-mile of chase. The stolen truck ended up smashing a sedan on Avenida Revolución without causing major damage. The occupants of the sedan were shocked by the daylight pursuit, but were left shaken without any bodily injury. The deputies came to find out that the thief was high on a combination of illicit drugs. The thief was screaming at the deputies and the medical crew that a cobra was spitting acid on his face. The cobra was causing his clothes to be set on fire while his heart was revving. Another reveler who knew him showed up to give some explanations to the authorities.

"I have known him for a few weeks. I have seen that he almost passed on his excessive drinking," said a young female reveler. "He was telling several people that he came down here to do what his parents and authorities in his hometown did not allow him to do."

"Where did he say he was from? What's his name?"

"I only heard his friends call him Bo. I do not know where he is from," answered the reveler.

"What did you see him drinking?"

"Everything and anything that he could pay for on the streets and on the beach. He downs booze, cocaine, and any synthetic drugs from China."

"Tell us more about the source of the synthetics. We found him driving naked. He was butt naked behind the wheel."

"That is not uncommon. On Avenida Revolución or anywhere else, if you have enough cash, you will even buy a lion."

"We have had several cases of overdose. We got the phone calls. Before arriving at the scene, the EMTs have been there trying to resuscitate them. In most cases, the death is the result of Fentanyl, Flakka, Molly, and a combination of those synthetics. These drugs destroying families and our young men."

"If you did not arrest this one, I am sure he would be one of the new statistics."

After detaining and taking this car thief, OD to jail, he was left there to dry out.

This was one of the thousands of incidents that would happen before the night was over. It would only take any observer less than one hour to hang out around a bar, a disco, or night club to witness the tragicomedy of life. Well-off young men and women who traveled here to drink and get lost. On most occasions, they did not bring any chaperones. They wanted to forget about their fear and pains.

They wanted to forget about the fast lifestyle of their homeland. They would never know about the danger that lurked around. The booze, sand, sun, and vodkas had a way of dumbing tourists down. While most beach fronts, hotels, and businesses are protected by a high police presence, the rest of the country, the interior of the country was not well protected to provide enough security.

Street vendors were hustling their merchandise on the beachfront. Each tourist they saw was an eventual sale. Some of them sold all of their merchandise. They returned home to get more to display or walk around. Street vendors let tourists bargain for the best prices. Ultimately, they knew the true price of their merchandise. They had already marked them up. Mafia and gang members also wanted a share of the business. They had already placed their own merchants in specific areas of the long beach area and Avenida Revolución. They were there to provide security for their own benefits. They were not ready to let intruders such as gang members and deported criminals take a slice of their established or burgeoning businesses.

"As long as I am not preventing my competitor to earn a living, I am fine here," said a merchant under his stall.

"Who is monitoring and providing your security?" asked a tourist who used to be a former US journalist before retiring in this enclave.

"It used to be bad here. But lately, there is a huge police presence here. We can now breathe. But the underground forces of darkness continue to function here. I cannot point fingers. I will continue to mind my own business."

"I feel safer here than most places in my home country," said the retired journalist.

"Lucky are you! You never knew when insecurity prevented us to earn a living on the streets. Avenida Revolución was not always like this. I will say it is a paradise now," said the street vendor.

"Back in the old days, I used to report about Spring Break. I was more concerned about having fun on the beach, the clubs, the bars, and the discos. Yes, I did encounter some tough guys, but they were all drunk."

"Yes, I was among the fun-looking guys on the long track of beach sand. But now I have kids and a family to take care of. I have to sell my products."

"I understand. I return to this corner of Baja to relax. Everything is easy to get as long as I stay in the tourist area. I have never had any problem around here."

"Well, I am happy for you. Please tell others to come to TJ. This place has greatly changed. The more tourists come to Baja California, the more I will sell my merchandise to take care of my family. I will not need to cross the border."

"Well, I will for sure. My friends love TJ. Those who have not been here are missing out. Mexicans are good people. They are not bad hombres as they are portrayed. They should be proud of themselves. I guess I wanted you to know that...."

"Well thanks very much. We hope that a day will come when our brothers and sisters will stay home to work. They would not have to be treated like trash on foreign soil. As long as the rich of our country continue to invest in our economy, we should advance," said the street vendor.

"To tell you the truth, I did not expect to hear such great words from you. I was under the impression that street vendors are all the same. You blow my mind today," said the former journalist.

"Well, right here, you will find street vendors who graduated from top Mexican universities. You will find even those who studied in the United States but could not stay there and decide to return to TJ. Street Vendors are business people. We are engaged in one of the oldest professions."

"I thought it was prostitution. Once again, I was wrong," said the former journalist with some sarcasm.

Both men took a few seconds of silence before laughing. Nearby, two ambulances showed up. The medical crew entered a multipurpose building whose main attraction was the bar with a great veranda overlooking the ocean. Two revelers were shot last night. To prevent tourists from getting scared, the bodies were stuffed in a back room until the deputies could accompany the medical crew and ambulances to pick them up. Eyewitnesses reported they were members of a competing cartel that were doing some reconnaissance. They wanted to take over the control of kickbacks and other dealings on the beach. Nobody could verify this information. And the deputies were not releasing any information either. They continued to conduct their investigation which could take weeks and months. By then, this will have been water under the bridge.

The bars, discos, and restaurants served lots of alcoholic beverages. Young revelers inhibited by cheap drugs, booze, and vodka could not differentiate between safety, security, and danger. Yet, some armed revelers did not mind displaying their weapons to the beautiful women who were parading the hotels, restaurants, discos, and bars. On any given day, there were enough guns, drugs such as crack cocaine, molly, beautiful women and enough drunk beach dudes ready to cause trouble. If it was not for the presence of deputies and police stationed on Avenida Revolución, the whole place would turn into a bloody wild west shootout. The beachfront restaurants were competing against each other. Their loud music could pierce any adults' ear drum. It appears there was nobody to monitor the noise level in town.

Chapter 8

Migrants and homeless decided to join Sister Petra and Sister Tetra in the large compound of the Traveling Sisters of the Higher Purpose Shelter. The two Sisters had been talking about this bonfire for a few days now. They wanted the migrants and homeless community to gather together to share stories about their trek across the Americas and the rest of the world. They also made sure to invite the amazing guests of the Sisters Restaurant without whose assistance sheltering and feeding the migrants and homeless population would be practically impossible. Parents accompanied their all-too-excited kids to the bonfire. By 8 Pm, The Sisters Restaurant guests arrived and started to mingle with the migrants and homeless.

On that moonlit night, the children were running around. They wanted the storytelling session to start. However, the adults continued to mingle. Then, it was up to the nuns to welcome everybody and introduce some of the storytellers.

"Welcome to this great bonfire! We are happy to see all of our guests here. Tonight, we will have lots of fun," said Sister Petra. "We will listen to stories from around the world. We are so blessed to have the world at our door. We have migrants from Africa, Asia, and Latin America. All of these migrants are trying to get to the United States. Unfortunately for many of them, crossing over to the U.S. has become very difficult. For two hours, we will reconnect with our inner soul. Storytelling exists everywhere."

It was Sister Tetra's turn to say a few words.

"We want to say thanks to all the parents who brought their children to this bonfire tonight. And we say thank you too to the kids who dragged their parents out of their bed tonight. Let me say thank you to all the business people of our community who have been supporting our ministry. You know who you are. I do not need to name any names."

"Let me introduce you to our first storyteller. His name is Tony. Tony will tell you more. Please be ready to listen to Tony's story. Clap your hands and scream," said Sister Petra.

Tony got onto the podium. Without taking any further ado, he started telling his story.

****

"The Horse Whisperer, The Bucking Donkeys, and The Horse Caravan"

"I remember the days and nights when I used to camp on my grandparents' horse farms. Growing up on a farm with many chores to engage in brings back the memories of some of my favorite activities. Getting up early to visit the stables and barns where some of the family's animals stayed was one of my many chores. As I grew older and knew how to take care of the various animals on the farms, the fun days and nights diminished. I always looked forward to spending time with my grandparents on the main house's porch at night where my favorite tea was served by my mother.

Sitting on the front porch overlooking the rolling green hills loaded with fruit trees and the Caribbean ocean, we took our time telling stories and sipping our tea at the end of the long day of work. After all, there was always so much to do on such a large farm with so many animals. From the days when I could only walk out to accompany my parents and grandparents, I enjoyed being out. I was an early riser. I got up early so I could smell the aroma of the nearby huge coffee plantations that the hills and valleys. No two mornings were the same. The crow of the roosters kept coming from the nearby neighbors' yards. The barking of the dogs were a clear sign of the strong walk of the mountain farmers carrying their crops on their head to the open-air Saturday market in town. Being the favorite grandson of both of my grandmothers, Claire Midi and Madame Antoinette, I received gifts and small bags full of rare fruits and vegetables grown way up deep in the mountains. It was a clear exchange between my grandmothers and their mountain friends who did not have the variety of fruits and vegetables grown close to the waterways and ocean. On many occasions, these mountain farmers could not stop because their loaded mules and donkeys passed so quickly in front of my grandparents' homes. Besides, they had to arrive at the market before the local farmers who will also sell their crops. It was a competition to find the best spots to raise their tents. As far as the workers of the town are concerned, it was on a first-come first-served basis. Needless to say that the heated competition gave rise to various conflicts and fights between the merchants.

I remember that my grandparents and father had to go into the market to provide some conflict resolution talk. Even the animals that brought all these varieties of crops down from the mountain got into some brouhaha too. The jackasses were the worse during the mating season. They would do anything to get out of stalls they occupied. They pushed down gates to run across town, destroying the hard-produced crops and causing a stampede of mules and donkeys. Most of the conflicts started when jackasses ran through the buzzing market at midday causing a havoc of all kinds of crops, olive oil, fish, corn, millet, rice, potatoes, and fruits.

"Oh no, stop your jackass! It's coming this way." yelled Tristan, a mountain merchant who was talking to her nearby neighbor. They did not get along because the rich inhabitants of the town often bought their merchandise from her tents.

"Are you talking to me? How many times have I told you not to disrupt me when I am taking care of my merchants?" responded Mène.

"I can say whatever I want to say. I cannot wait for the day when you will be robbed and lose your money to fill your tent with merchandise," said Tristan, a mountain merchant who was well-known across town for her fights. She came from a large family of pickpockets.

"Well, thanks for letting me know that you will send your husband or son to rob me. Just so you know, if anything happens to me, my husband and the local authorities already know you have been making threats against me and my family," replied Mène.

"I have told you to get the hell away from me. I'd rather have another merchant around here. Leave so I can have your tent spot. If you cannot leave on your own, I will help you."

"Tristan, you have such a beautiful name but you are a devil. I am not afraid of satan or the devil. God is with me, I will not fear any evil."

"Mène, you know where I come from. If you were smart, you would be careful with what you say. My roots are deep. If you keep talking like this, I will sell your soul to the devil."

"Tristan, my soul is well protected by the love of Jesus. If God is with me, I shall not fear your devil. You need God's love. Why don't you come to church with me on a Sunday morning?"

Tristan saw her favorite consumer walking by. She started making small talk with the consumer to try to get her to stop by her tent.

"What happened, my main buyer? I have not seen you lately," said Tristan.

"Well, I went on vacation with my employer for two months. We went to Plaine du Nord and Milot," replied Asefi who was a beautiful marabou with long black hair and blue eyes.

"Do not tell me that your employer and his family have been to the St Jacques' festival in the North every year."

"Yes. This was the first time I was able to accompany them. Usually, the family would travel either to South America or Miami."

"Well, you look great. Have you found a boyfriend yet?" asked Tristan. "It may be time to go out with one of my sons or brothers."

"Tristan, you never stop trying to hook me up with your family member. I want to wait till I complete my education. Your family members are too complicated."

"Asefi, do not pay attention to the lies and gossip those crazy people are telling about my amazing sons and brothers."

"What do you have to show me today? I am looking for some fresh watercress, beats, and eggs."

"You know I have everything that you need. I will give you the best price too. Are you shopping for the family? Or for your own parents?"

"I am shopping for both," replied Asefi who walked to the area where fresh watercress and other vegetables were displayed.

"What are you going to cook tonight for the families?"

"I intend to make some French cooking tonight. The watercress is going to be part of the soup. I will need to get a head of pig. I will cook it till tomorrow afternoon. I do not know if I told you about this before. I have been working with a family whose roots go back to Spain, France and Africa. So from time to time, I surprise the kids with something from the old country."

"No. I never knew that. They must pay you well. You are a very great chef around town," said Tristan.

"Thanks, Tristan. I attended le Cordon Bleu Paris where I studied at Hautes Etudes du Goût. In other words, I have been hired to improve their French gastronomy."

"Asefi, I enjoy seeing you. Pick whatever you want here. I will give you a good price," said Tristan who was getting busier and busier entertaining other clients.

Not too far from Tristan and Mène's shops a new brouhaha was taking place. The merchants were chasing a group of thieves who were trying to escape with some cash. They started beating their pan or casserole to create as much noise as possible. They wanted to warn other merchants who were seating and selling their merchandise at the far-away corners of the open-air market. A group of gendarmes or police officers managed to detain two thieves, but the rest escaped among the crowd.

"Thieves! Thieves! Thieves!"

And when I was able to ride my first horse, I did not hesitate to jump on its back so I could go explore the large farms. More importantly, I wanted to be closer to the farm hands who appeared to know each one of these animals very well.

From where the main farm house stood on top of a hill full of fruit trees on both sides, I could hear the crashing of the Caribbean waves. In the early morning hours, I enjoyed entering the coffee plantations to listen to the chirping of the birds that came early to check the red juicy beans. In those days, it was easier to travel to the coffee plantations on the back of a donkey. It was the time when there was a true dry season and rainy season. It was also the time when fruits were in abundance, especially during the summer. It was hot but the rivers and the ocean were nearby. The flatlands were not intact because the treeless mountain mud did not destroy them. The mountains and hills were covered with beautiful fruit trees. There was no inundation. The streets and rivers did not become muddy. It was the time when children could play outside without any fear. It was the time when there was enough security, safety, food on the table, and hope for a better tomorrow. It was also the time when parents did not have to abandon their children by leaving them behind. It was the time when parents did not have to go on a multi-country march to find a better life somewhere else. It was the time when grandparents only had time to play with their grandchildren, but not to raise them because their parents are breaking their back in places that care less about them. Needless to say it had nothing to do with our current time when we have to cross hills and mountains, desert and rivers to go to the north. Thank you for listening to my story," said Tony who received a standing ovation.

Some of the Mexican business people and other guests took his name and promised to stay in touch with him.

Sister Petra took the microphone. "This was one of the stories from this year's Storytelling series. This is just the beginning. It's going to be more fun. Our next guest is a special author and researcher. He will share with us the first chapter of his second novel. Are we not lucky to have the best of the best among us here tonight? Let's give him a warm welcome."

Alfonso walked onto the podium and started to speak.

"You call Mr. Alfonso an unscrupulous coyote, a nasty people-smuggler who should be thrown into jail. You should call me an entrepreneur, a successful author and writer, a reporter, a business man, a survivor who understands how the underworld economy works. I am Alfonso, born and raised in New York City, right in Bedford-Stuyvessant also known as Bed-Stuy, Brooklyn. I am a New Yorker with deep roots in the Caribbean and Central America. Pushed by the 1970 and 1980s violence of Guatemala, Honduras, and El Salvador, my mother's parents came to Florida. Later on, they settled in New York to reach the American Dream.

That's where my Haitian-Dominican father ran into this beautiful, gorgeous Maya Quiche woman who was studying to be a nurse at CUNY, City University of New York. He fell in love with her. And the rest is my story. Needless to say that every summer, I would go to volunteer either in Haiti, Dominican Republic or Guatemala, Honduras, and El Salvador! My summer vacation became an open-door university for me. Every year, vacation became my escape to a world where people are different and happy despite their poverty and abuse by whoever was in power in any of these countries. In Haiti, I survived Papa Duck and Baby Duck. And In Central America, I witnessed and survived the guerilla warfare and the exploitation and racism of the elites against the indigenous majority.

Those days, I could do only one thing: observe and learn from the various indigenous groups who were full of wisdom. I knew that I would be able to help them some day. Even if it is only by telling their stories to the greater mass in the world. "The country of Guatemala currently ranks as the second most unequal in Latin America and the Caribbean, surpassed only by Haiti. The wealthiest 10 percent of

Guatemalans earn 47.5 percent of national income, while less than 20 percent is allocated to the poorest 60 percent. Indigenous Guatemalans, who represent the majority of the country's population, account for an estimated 80 percent of Guatemala's poor. Roughly one-quarter of them live in conditions of extreme poverty."

Yes, I was truly fortunate to have been born in New York City. My frequent visits to the Caribbean and Central America, especially to these countries, showed me that people who look like my mother and my father whose skin color and blood I carry in my veins are still suffering in Haiti, the Dominican Republic, Guatemala, Honduras, and El Salvador. And in the past few decades, the powerful drug cartels, gang violence, and extreme poverty are still pushing them to leave their homeland. The only difference is that this time and unlike my grandparents and parents, these new victims will not be lucky to find easy refuge in places such as Los Angeles, New York, Florida, Texas and elsewhere.

Back in the 1980s, I grew up in an area where young people were afraid of walking at night and where mothers were crying and praying for the safety of their sons and daughters. I grew up with the few guys who survived the street urban violence of Bed-Stuy, Chelsea and Hell's Kitchen, Brooklyn Heights. That's before gentrification has taken over and brought great changes to these places. Murders, robberies, and burglaries were common in places that were once considered idyllic and safe family neighborhoods. My parents were praying for me and my siblings, day in and day out. They were not sure I would make it. If I did not get cut down by violent gang activities in those days, I might have been choked down by the New York City police or NYPD. Then, the worst thing arrived on the streets. Drugs. Then, my parents and school counselors started telling me to stay away from drug dealers, the corner street vendors who might want to use me as a mule. The fight against drugs pushed by the then administration ended up sending more African-American, Jamaican, Puerto-Rican and other ethnic group members to prison than their European descent drug users.

I grew up with Jay-Z before he reached his current stardom. And he remains one of the most famous sons of Bed-Stuy, Brooklyn. His story is that of a young man who found the right path to survive and live a prosperous life in the American society. Music was his path and still is. I also grew up in a New York City where Mike Tyson was a young man roaming over Brownsville before finding boxing as his way out of the street violence. My playgrounds were Huntspoint, Greenwich Village and Meatpacking District, and Flatiron which had a horrible reputation for prostitution in particular and crime in general. With easy means of public transportation that New York is known for all over the world, I was able to go downtown and Uptown in a few Subway rides. I started observing and writing about the large cacophony of people going up and down Manhattan. I observed people who were waiting in line all the time. I started thinking about a business idea that could meet their needs. Frankly, most of these rich people did not want to stay in line on a rainy day and night.

Do not get me wrong about what gentrification has done for NYC. Gentrification has brought great value to local real estate. Rundown apartment complexes have become $ million condos. In places such as Clinton Hill, rapper's hood has soon become yuppie haven. I am not the one to forget the early street performances and successful rap songs of Biggie (Notorious B.I.G) Smalls. We were about the same age when he used to bag groceries, shoot dice, and sell dope at the corner of Fulton Street. His pounding beats would elevate him to the stardom. Unfortunately, he was cut down by bullets, gunned down in Las Vegas in 1997 at such an early age and right in his prime days of stardom.

Such was the fast-paced life on the street. Now, thanks to the efforts of various NYC authorities, young entrepreneurs, African-American, Caribbean, Central and South American and European business people, families can walk on the streets without the fear of being mugged in bright daylight. Drug dealers may take a back seat these days.

On a few occasions, I had to take a taxi. Taking New York City's cabs has become my street classroom. Everything that I wanted to learn about people in general and New York, in particular, was made possible by the various conversations I had with cab drivers. On a few occasions, I found myself making it a habit of taking cabs and the subway in order to learn more about the various groups of people coming from all over the world. The taxi drivers came from all ethnic, religious and socio-economic backgrounds. Their most common points were that they cursed a lot. And they never failed to tell me stories about when New York City's muggers would rob them after pointing a gun to their throat. In those days and even now, doctors were taxi drivers. Those who were college professors in their homeland ended up being cab drivers a few weeks or months after arriving in New York. I will never forget the stories of a Kenyan cab driver who was a king in waiting in his homeland. He stated that he was making more money driving a taxi here than what his parents were making back in Kenya. The difference is that he felt safe when he goes back home to participate in some annual ceremonies. "Yes, there is a lot of money to make in America, but the lifestyle is shitty," said that cab driver who will eventually become the king/chief of his village. Other cab drivers are also great writers and poets who did not hesitate to share their work with me. Paying a fare was like paying to attend the best university that money can send a young man to. These writers/cab drivers had to work to feed their family. They work days and nights to be able to send money back to their home country. Their parents, children and wives depend on the remittances. They send money to pay for their kids' education, to take care of their parents, and to build their dream home.

Over the years, in some developing countries of the world, remittances make up massive proportions of national income. And

I started thinking about the number of worldwide migrants which would form the 5th most populated country after China, India, America, and Indonesia. According to the World Bank's Migration and Remittances Factbook, over 200 million people migrate from their country of birth to foreign lands. The stories these cab drivers were telling me made me take a look at the top beneficiaries of remittances as far as the amount of money received by these countries. Bear in mind that remittances are private cash flows, typically from a migrant abroad to a family at home. These countries are: India, China, Mexico, Philippines, Nigeria, France, Egypt, Germany, Pakistan, and Bangladesh. More than $23 billion is sent to Mexico every year from the U.S. alone. More than $60.7 billion is sent back to China every year by Chinese Migrant workers. Indian migrant workers send more than $61 billion every year in remittance funds. The last data showed that $24 billion is sent back to Philippines every year by migrant workers. So here we are being stuck in TJ, Mexicali and other border towns.

Considering how much money migrants send back home, I wanted to take a look at a few countries whose citizens pushed by economic, criminal, poverty, violence, and abuse factors end up migrating to other countries, specially, the United States of America and Canada. After all, I have gone to most cantinas and local shops that serve specific ethnic groups and witnessed the large group of people visiting to send money back home. In general, migrants send home three times more money than countries receive in development aid. I have also taken a look at the pull factors of countries such as the United States. They include better jobs, any kind of field and manual works, better schools for their children, better housing even if it includes apartments located in unsafe neighborhoods, ghettos and barrios. The ragged apartments of Western and Florence in South Central LA may form a temporary point for most immigrants who may end up moving to where they can find good jobs and housing. For sure, most immigrants will soon learn about Skid Row's crime. And they'll want to flee it as soon as they can."

At the end of this speech, Alfonso received a standing ovation from the bonfire crowd. Most of the guests were asking him questions about New York's street life. Most migrants found him to be very reliable. Alfonso grew up on the streets of New York. The migrants who were stuck on the Mexico-US border towns wanted to listen to somebody like Alfonso.

By the time most of the guests had a chance to ask their questions, it was almost midnight.

As the crowd was mingling around, two little girls were accompanied by Sister Tetra to the podium.

"I have two young girls who have been looking for their parents. They have been in our shelter for the past 2 months," said Sister Tetra. "A raid in the jungle separated them from their parents. They arrived her with other migrants from Congo. They are still traumatized."

"What languages do they speak?" asked a few voices from the audience.

"I have seen several Haitian migrants talking to them. They must speak French or Haitian Creole," replied another voice.

"What are their names?"

"They are Carline and Rose. They are shocked by the events of the trek. We take good care of them even when we cannot talk with them. If the parents do not come to claim them, we will adopt them. Sister Petra and I have been talking about it."

"Here is Carline," Sister Petra said as she introduced her to the audience. "Here is Rose."

It was at that point that Christèle looked at them. She moved to the front of the podium to ask them a few questions.

"Which country did you come from? De quel pays êtes-vous? Ki kote nou soti?" asked Christèle as she approached closer and closer.

"Nous sommes d'Haiti. Nou soti Ayiti. We are from Haiti," replied Carline, a very extrovert girl.

"Nous venons de Les Cayes. Nou soti Okay," clarified Rose.

By then, Christèle realized that the two beautiful girls were from Haiti. They had the same blood as she did. She was determined to help them, but she needed to ask them more questions.

"When was the last time you were with your parents?" asked Christèle.

"Well, we were together in Brazil. For many days and nights, we were together as we were crossing many difficult countries," replied Carline.

"Then, we were almost lost in the jungle. We ended up being chased by some gang members or drug cartels. Our parents had told us to remain together even if they were forced to run in a different direction. That was the last time we saw them," said Rose who felt comfortable to tell her story. She was happy to be able to talk to somebody who knew where she came from. Until then, Christèle did not want to reveal much about them. She knew them more they could have thought.

"Which group of migrants were you with?" asked Christèle.

"A family from Congo took us. They speak French. I heard them speaking other languages too," said Rose.

"Do you know what happened to your parents?" asked Christèle.

"No. People are saying that many migrants are held as captives until their family can pay the ransom. My parents are not rich. They do not have family members who could pay large sums of money either," said Carline.

It was at that time that Christèle decided to reveal herself to the two girls. She realized that she needed.

"I spent some time in Chile. From Chile, I went to Brazil to launch my food business. That was way before the summer Olympic games. I cooked Haitian meals for the workers. When I could not make any money, I decided to take my chance. Because a lot of people were migrating to the US."

"Is that how you end up being here with us?"

"Well, yes and no. I should have been in the US now, but I lost my paperwork. Things did not work out for me," said Christèle.

"Did you know my parents?" asked Rose.

"Well, I did not know your parents, but I knew people you know."

"Can you give me one name?" asked Carline.

"Viviana," replied Christèle.

"She is my godmother's mother. I used to go to her house to spend time with my godmother. She is a nice woman," said Rose.

"Viviana and the judge used to give us presents," said Carline.

"How did you know Viviana? Are you from our hometown?"

"Well, Viviana was worried about you because your godmother kept asking her to find out about what happened to you."

"Well, our parents left the country without telling anybody. They obtained a visa to go to Brazil because they were promised a job," said Carline.

"Wow, it's a small world." Both girls were smiling. They were happy to know somebody who knew their friends.

"How about a boy you used to play with? What happened to him?" asked Christèle.

"We lost contact with him. His name is TiGrimo. When we left, we did not say anything to anybody. His parents may have left for Bahamas. It was the time when all Haitians were migrating. The quake and hurricanes were chasing us," said Carline.

When Sister Petra and Sister Tetra realized that the girls were comfortable talking to Christèle, they moved away to talk to a few more guests.

"We would like to thank our special guests tonight. A special thank from Sister Petra and me goes to our two speakers tonight. We will try to find other speakers for you. We do not know how long you will be here in these border towns. We know that any literary Bonfire event will be useful to you," said Sister Tetra as the crowd was dispersing.

"Yes, we would like more such great speakers. Please find them for us. We thank you, Sisters, for organizing this bonfire tonight," said many bonfire attendees among the departing audience.

Using WhatsApp, Christèle sent a message to Viviana back home. "I have found the two girls, but their parents may have been kidnapped or disappeared during the journey."

Viviana was all too happy to transfer this message to her daughter studying in the capital. She forwarded the same message to her daughter who knew these two girls very well.

"Christèle, thank you for this amazing message. How did you find them," asked Viviana who was so happy that her husband Judge Balthazar came down from his study room to celebrate wither.

"At least two Haitian girls were rescued! How many others from Pestel, Tiburon, and Port-Salut perished while trying to find life on planet Earth?" Judge Balthazar groaned. "That's the situation of the country. Our fellow men and women are resorting to being jungle travelers."

Viviana stayed in communication with Christèle.

"How did you find yourself stranded with all those global travelers in Mexicali?"

"No, I am stranded in Tijuana. They called it TJ too. That's where I found the girls during a storytelling at a bonfire last night."

"Based on the international news, it looks like there are a lot of Haitians on the border towns," texted Viviana on WhatsApp.

"You are right. You can encounter Asians, Africans, Central Americans, and Europeans in the border towns such as TJ, Mexicali, Nogales, El Paso, Calexico, Tecate, and Reynosa etc." wrote Christèle. "TJ and Mexicali are the places I have been thus far. The faces of the world can be found right in these two places."

"How long are you going to be in TJ?" asked Viviana, sitting on the front porch of her home. That's where she has been able to find out what's going on in her country, from the capital to the provinces and the rest of the world.

"I cannot tell you. Nobody can tell you how it will take us to be here. The only thing that is certain is the sun rises up and goes down every day. All of us, migrants, have become used to spending days and nights outside. It's like we are camping all the time."

"What do the women do? What do you do? How do you spend your days?" asked Viviana.

"Well, I do not stay in one spot. I have been using my skills to survive. I approached some restaurant owners. I strike with them a deal they cannot refuse," answered Christèle.

"What kind of deal, Chris? You are a beautiful Haitian woman. You have class," asked Viviana, surprised to find out that her best friend stayed busy despite the flow of migrants who have been competing to survive.

"I a Madan Sara. I know how to cook. I know Haitians like to eat their own home-cooked meals. So for a decent pay, I volunteer to cook Haitian meals in those restaurants. I am hoping that I can make a living in this country. I doubt that Haitians will leave TJ. Immigration rules are tighter in the North. The new US president is not opening the doors to let people like us enter. We have to make a living where we can," said Christèle.

"You have not told me how you spend your days and nights in these circumstances, Chris?" said Viviana.

"I remain busy. Before finding these two girls, I used to go to the bars when I had some extra spending money. Now, I have my kids and these kids to take care of. I like going to the beach too."

"Thanks for informing me. I read that there are a lot of deported people in TJ and Mexicali."

"Yes, there are a lot of drug addicts too. The deported could not afford to go back to their community. They were saying that the closer they remain to the US, the more they have a chance to cross the border.

It's complete desperation. There are Central Americans who are running away from gang members. There are Asians who cannot afford to travel back to their country of origin. They remain in Tijuana. They stay in cheap hotels. There are $1 a night hotels. Heroin, cocaine, MJ, Fentanyl, Oxycontin, Valium, Percodan, Codeine, Viagra, birth control pills, fertility drugs, Molly and synthetic drugs are used in those places. They are saving their money to buy more drugs. They even sleep on the sidewalk on some occasions. Most of them are not Mexicans. They are people who are trying to survive. They have no chance of ever making it to the US. Even if they had an appointment to plead their case, they would be high."

"Wow, that must be very serious over there!" exclaimed Viviana.

"Yes, if you can name it, you will find it on the border. There are buses of tourists that arrive to shop in those Drug Discounters. They have bright signs of neon that attract the young as well as the adults. Some Mexicans call it Gringolandia. That's where you find the young painkillers poppers who are smiling and laughing idiotically on the beach and at the bars on Avenida Revolución. They can be high that they pee on themselves. They come to TJ or Mexicali loaded with cash to drink mojito, Tequila Sunrise, and Chili or Mandarin Margarita."

"Do you go to those places to dance or to drink?"

"Well, I go to those places to watch the waste of rich people. They bring lots of money to be wasted in a few days. I like watching the street drunkards and beggars. I go there to dance. What else to do in those places? Everything is so transitional. Nothing is there forever. People seem to be in transit."

"You are in transit too. The mass of humanity is there with you," wrote Viviana who decided to record her WhatsApp messages to send to Christèle.

"Viviana, I can tell you that wealth and abject poverty collide in this place. You can see the superstars coming in, surrounded by bodyguards. At the same time, you can see the narco lords as well as the narco entrepreneurs driving in fancy cars, carrying their gold-plated chains weapons and ammunitions. Viviana, I have not seen them, but the locals have been saying that they travel here to have fun or do business. I hope I do not have to cross path with them."

"How long will it take you to show up at your appointment with the US officials?"

"Well, I have obtained an appointment date thus far. By the way things are going these days, it may be months before I get to plead my case before the officials. In the meantime, people are getting deported. For a few months now, some of the migrants are getting deported to their homeland. Considering that many of these people sold their homes, livestock, even borrowed money to get on this journey, I do not see how they can go back to be even poorer. That's why some of them decide to stay in the borderland. I tease some of them that we are ally sniffing and praying for the opportunity to go there to work."

"Chris, you never stop making jokes. You are still funny," Viviana said, laughing.

"What else can we do? What else can I say? I have already done my share of crying. I could become sad, but sadness will ameliorate my situation."

"You can pray and meditate. I will keep you in my prayers. By the way, the Catholic Church that was destroyed by the 2010 quake has been rebuilt. There are 3 masses a day. The priest is very busy."

"Yes. Thanks for your prayers. I am praying for strength and courage. It looks like most migrants have to wait for the current president to complete his mandate or term. Maybe a new president will work on the immigration issues. People who are stranded far from their homeland will be given a chance to cross."

"As I often say, there is better place than home. Your country may be poor, but it is yours. The only problem is the lack of security. I am hoping the criminals will give Haiti a chance to move forward. The gang members should think about the future. Those who were deported from foreign lands because of their criminal activities need to give the country a chance," Viviana said.

"Thank you very much, Viv. I will continue to depend on your prayers. Talking about prayers, I have to go to church service tonight. There a few pastors who have been traveling with us. In the past, pastors used to have a better life, but things change. Some of them lie too much," said Christèle.

"Do not say that. In every religion, the men of the robes are not all saints," Viviana declared. "You just have to take a look at what our priests have been doing."

"I do not know if I had told you about the two nuns who own this shelter. They organized the bonfire's storytelling event last night. Some locals have been saying they are fake nuns. As for most of us, migrants, they are almost saints. They are so loving and kind to us."

"Chris, I am very happy that you can see the difference. There are good nuns, good priests, and good pastors. At the same time, there are some bad ones too."

"Do not worry. I will keep an eye on those two girls. Greetings to you and your family! Thanks for your encouragement and prayers."

"Before you know it, God will open some doors for you. Whether you stay in Mexico or travel to the US, God will show you the way. You will be able to make a living. Thanks for everything."

"Please send my news to my parents," asked Christèle.

"I will. Keep me informed on WhatsApp."

"I will for sure. I have just heard about the news of a fire in an overcrowded shelter. More than a dozen of the migrants perished. The firefighters continue to save lives. The ambulance and EMTs are going up and down."

"Be safe. That's life drama. Take care of yourself."

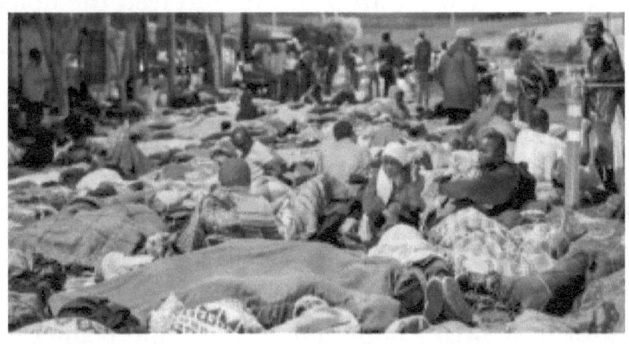

The next morning, Christèle woke up early and was determined to go volunteer some time at the Sisters' Restaurant. She had realized how much the two Sisters have done to make migrants' life more bearable in a foreign country. On her way to the restaurant, she could not walk past the immense ocean of colors that was being displayed right in front her. Adults as well as children from Africa, Asia, and Latin America were sleeping right on the street next to an overcrowded shelter. Christèle realized that some of them could not sleep. Others did not care about where they were. They had just arrived from the jungle and were too tired to ask for much more comfort. All the motels they could afford were already taken. When Mother Nature calls, one cannot do anything. These migrants had to sleep. They had to rest. Then, they will wake up to find some warm meals to eat. Christèle wanted to be one of the many people who had to feed those hungry travelers. In addition, she knew she would see Carline and Rose. She wanted to make sure that they were well cared for. She did not have any doubt that Sister Petra and Sister Tetra would treat them well. By volunteering in their kitchen, she wanted to pay back for the solidarity and welfare they offered to that mass of homeless and migrants.

Once more, the Sisters' Restaurant was open early. The breakfast crowd of rich business people and government workers figured out that they could help others by contributing to that ministry. They could not miss their reservation made in advance. In front of this mass migration, they did not mind paying a little bit more to feed the homeless and migrants they saw every day. The two Sisters appreciated any assistance they could get.

"Christèle, welcome to our restaurant. Thanks for wanting to be part of the feeding crew."

"Good morning, Sisters Petra and Tetra! I had some free time today. I could not stay in my motel room without doing something worthwhile."

"Good for us, Chris! I hope you do not mind being called Sister Chris!"

"Not all. Some people, some of my friends used to call me Sisi Chris," responded Christèle.

"We need some help in the kitchen. I have heard that you are a good cook."

"I am ready to do anything you want. I will wash dishes, clean the floor, and do anything else."

Sisi Chris or Christèle disappeared into the busy kitchen where the chefs and waitresses were giving and receiving orders.

Christèle was very happy to be part of this amazing crew of volunteers. There were so many things she could learn.

The paying customers enjoyed their breakfast and lunch. With a full belly, they knew they were footing the bill for the refugees, homeless and migrants' dinner in the evening. Sister Tetra and Sister Petra tapped into another source of revenues because their little restaurant became so popular that priests, high Mexican government officials, entrepreneurs, industrialists, and Narco lords came in disguise to eat their breakfast and lunch at the Sisters' Restaurant. They wanted to do something and figured out that the two Sisters' ministry gave them an opportunity to tackle this global mass migration.

In the evening, Christèle witnessed how the restaurant treated its poor migrants and homeless. There was no difference between the breakfast/lunch services and the dinner offered to people like her. That was compassion and act of kindness in action.

The same evening, she went to pray in one of the churches, currently overcrowded with faithful celebrants praying for hours at a time. The preacher was preaching a sermon on wealth and prosperity. Christèle wanted to be hopeful. So were the other migrants.

She knelt, raised her hands, and cried to God.

"O God, you know why I am here. You are the only one who can open hardened hearts. You are above all the earthly power and governments. You dominate the whole world. You can make men and women tremble in a few seconds. I witnessed your power over the years of my life," Christèle was crying all along. "You can open closed doors. O God, do not let me perish in this place. Use me as your tool to get things done. Protect me as I travel in this patriarchal world. Show me the way and lead me to success and the 'Promised Land' wherever it can be!"

The noise, worship, and prayers of the migrants could be heard miles away. African, Asian, and Haitian prayer warriors surprised the residents of this ravine. In the past, way before those migrants from Congo and Latin America started crossing over the Mexican soil, the number of worshippers or church attendees could be counted on one hand. However, the ministry leaders never lost faith. And they were not surprised by the number of migrants sent to their doors. The small church in the ravine opened its doors to the refugees, migrants and homeless. And all those people continued to pray for a miracle. They wanted to find jobs to take care of their family members left behind. They wanted to go wherever they can find decent paying jobs.

With drums, clapping of hands, hymn singing, the members of the little church that could started attracting festival goers such as cowboys and vendors. "People have to live off bread and water." The street vendors were pushing their cart from the cheap motels to the churches where hungry worshippers needed food. When they could not sell on credit, the street vendors reminded them of the meals being served at the Sisters' Restaurant in the evening.

The sun rises once again. And it goes down for more than 4 years. The sun and moon stood still in their places. And so did the earth, harvest, brooks, birds, and sea...

Review:

"Super Survivors: Citizens of the World and Planet Earth / Super Sobrevivientes: Ciudadanos del Mundo y del Planeta Tierra" is a memoir of survival across parts of the old and new worlds. It is also the story of loss, pain, suffering, and survival. It is the story of two girls who survived the 2010 quake and 2016 hurricane Matthew only to embark on a journey with their parents through many Central and South American countries, especially the Darien Gap. Carline and Rose survived the catastrophic natural disasters and followed their parents to Brazil which they left a few months after. Their journey took them to the jungle of South and Central Americas, crossed many countries only to find themselves separated from their parents after a raid in the jungle. Will they ever get reunited with their parents? Who will take care of them during the rest of the journey to the North? Will they ever make it to the borderland? When and if they do make it, will they arrive at the Tijuana / San Ysidro Port of Entry?"

The immigration policies changed after the November 2016 election. A new president was elected in the USA. How long will the mass of African, Asian, and Latin American migrants be stranded in Tijuana, Mexicali, Tecate, Nogales, and other border towns?

Will Carline and Rose find a Good Samaritan to feed and shelter them until they have an appointment to plead their case?

With a new administration on the north, more and more migrants may finally realize that the American dream can be found on the other side of the border.

Did you love *Super Survivors: Citizens of the World and Planet Earth - Super Sobrevivientes: Ciudadanos del Mundo y del Planeta Tierra*? Then you should read *Hail to the King of Sneakers: Michael Jordan Nike Air Jordan Retro Time (A social media-loaded, marketing campaign, success story)*[1] by Kevin Levin and Charles Desmangles!

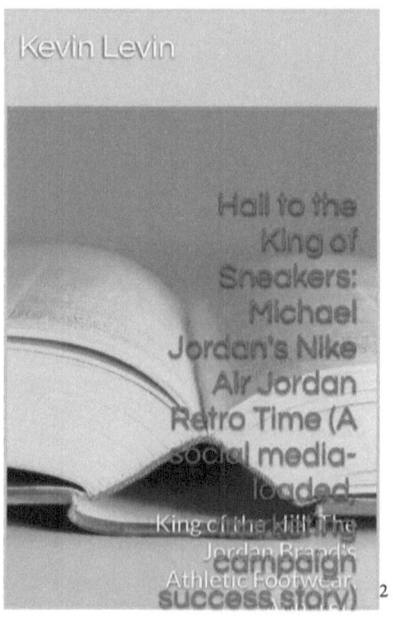

"Hail to the King of Sneakers:Michael Jordan's Nike Air Jordan Retro Time (A Social Media-loaded Marketing Campaign Success Story)" is an ebook about the history of Michael Jordan, a superhero, superstar basketball player who ended up becoming a great businessman after his retirement.It's also the story of sneaker collectors who did not mind staying in line to be able to buy a few pairs of his shoes.Over the years, superstar Michael Jordan has become a sacred hero.He was thought to have superhuman powers.In this ebook, you will read about the

1. https://books2read.com/u/bOaaPg

2. https://books2read.com/u/bOaaPg

shopping incidents, Michael's business advice, and hard-working skills.You will also read about the shoe empire he ends up building and the standout players who are part of his brand.

Michael Jordan produces shoes for his fans and consumers of all age group.In his mind, kids are his future markets.Find out where he got started and what he had to do to build this luxury shoe empire.From the school of hard knocks to various business textbooks and the key questions he had to ask, you will find out he was a determined player and businessman who wants to make a difference in this world.

Also by J C Doyle

Super Survivors: Citizens of the World and Planet Earth - Super Sobrevivientes: Ciudadanos del Mundo y del Planeta Tierra

Watch for more at www.josephjcharles.com.

Also by Kevin Levin

BestBusinessEbooks

Hail to the King of Sneakers: Michael Jordan Nike Air Jordan Retro Time (A social media-loaded, marketing campaign, success story)

Education Ebooks

Haiti's Hidden Treasures - Trezò Kache PeyidAyiti – Les Trésors Cachés d'Haïti

Hail to the New True Kings of Sneakers: Michael Jordan's Sneaker Empire, Lebron James, Kevin Durant's Sneaker Empire - Focus on Lebron James

Romance Language Publisher

Learn Creole Very Slowly – Aprendan Creole Despacito – Aprann Kreyòl Toudousman

Standalone

Super Survivors: Citizens of the World and Planet Earth - Super Sobrevivientes: Ciudadanos del Mundo y del Planeta Tierra

Watch for more at kevinlevinebooks.blogspot.com.

About the Author

J C Doyle is a Haitian-American writer who survived the dictatorship of Papa and Baby Doc. He had to come to the United States to pursue his higher studies. J C Doyle is interested in writing about the Haitian diaspora in the United States, Canada, Mexico, Chile, France, and anywhere in the world. Lately he has been focusing his travel writings on the plight of the global migrants' crisis. He also writes about the borderland, the border of countries such as Mexico and the US etc. He contributes articles and writings to the site below.

Read more at www.josephjcharles.com.

About the Publisher